Tomorrow...

What It Will
Be Like

Tomorrow ...

What It Will Be Like

by Herbert W. Armstrong

EVEREST HOUSE
Publishers   *New York*

Contents

Tomorrow...

What It Will
Be Like

1

Three World Views—Only One is Going to Happen!

YOU DON'T HAVE TO BELIEVE IT! IT WILL happen, regardless. It is sure—the world's only sure hope. This advance good news of tomorrow is as certain as the rising of tomorrow's sun.

Humanity won't bring it about—it is going to be done to us. Humanity is going to be forced to be happy—to enjoy world peace—to see universal abundance and joy fill the earth.

Utopia? Why not. Why should it be an imaginary or impossible pipe-dream? There is a cause for today's world chaos and threat of human extinction. That cause will be supplanted by that which will bring a utopia that is real, that is successfully functioning!

Why today's world evils? How will they be ended?

What will cause this world to erupt into peace, and plenty? How will such incredible changeover be brought about?

And what will this world *tomorrow* be like? How will it be governed? Who will rule?

You are going to take a sober look at the conditions, facts, causes and trends in today's sick, sick world.

You are going to read what world leaders, scientists, technologists and educators say about today's trends, and what they envision for the next decade or two.

And then you will be given a surprising, excited look into what is certain in the transformed world *tomorrow*, what really is ahead—and why.

Today there are three views—two widely held by world leaders. Only one is going to happen. And it's the best big news ever reported in the history of mankind. What is actually going to be the outcome of all this, for our frenetic, entertainment-crazed, gadget-buying, yet chaotic, divided and sick world, is something totally unseen by statesmen, scientists, educators, and world leaders.

What World Leaders Expect

The two most widely held views are divergent ones—paradoxically pointing in opposite directions.

Many world leaders now expect—though they probably don't dwell on the thought—that nuclear destruction eventually, perhaps soon, will erase human life from this earth.

Besides nuclear annihilation, there are at least five other means by which mankind could be destroyed from off the face of the globe: chemical warfare, biological warfare, overpopulation and resulting famine, disease epidemics, and environmental pollution.

Consider these facts: Human life is sustained by air,

water, and food. Today man is polluting his life-sustaining supply of these three necessities at a fast-accelerating rate. Air pollution, filling the air with gasses, smoke, smog, fallout from nuclear test explosions, and fluorocarbons from aerosol spray cans, not only threatens man, but renders plant life sick. Many rivers and lakes worldwide have been so seriously polluted that the water supply in many places is reaching a crisis stage. Man has depleted and ruined the soil out of which food must grow. Artificial fertilizers, poisonous sprays, and erosion caused by floods have robbed vegetables, grains and fruits of life-sustaining minerals and vitamins. Food factories have further extracted these vital elements out of grains, rice, sugar, in the greed for profits. Add to these the worldwide revolution in the weather—droughts and floods—resulting in mass starvations in some parts of the world, and widespread epidemics of disease. During the past 50 years in Africa, India and South America alone, weather and environmental damage has caused the loss of over one million square kilometers of agricultural land.

If all these fast-accelerating evils do not destroy humanity soon, the experts say the population explosion will. According to United Nations studies, world population at the end of this century will increase another 1.8 billion over the present four billion, bringing the total to nearly six billion people! At that time—just two decades from now—China and India will each have populations of over one billion.

Statistics further reveal that world population is increasing by some 76 million annually, which would lead to a doubling of world population to over 8 billion by the year 2013. And projections say that a century from now, a full 12 billion people would be crowding the earth.

Even now, with our population of 4 billion, nearly 500 million are gravely undernourished. As global population soars, the imbalance of human numbers and rapidly dwindling resources threatens to become even further aggravated. If the world cannot now adequately care for 4 billion, just how will it cope with 6 billion . . . or 8 billion . . . or 12 billion?

Leading scientists look at this world picture, and say they are frankly frightened. They warn us that man's only hope lies in the admittedly impossible—that the nations form a super *world government*, capable of unitedly acting on these problems on a global scale before it is too late. But the nations, hostile against one another, could never form such a government. And the humans then in authority would be no more able to cope with all these nonmilitary evils that threaten the extinction of mankind than present leaders.

This widely held view of the future offers no hope.

The Magic World of Science

Then, paradoxically, science and technology has dangled before our eyes a glittering, glamour-world of their making. It was to be a fantastic, push-button dreamworld of "the three Ls"—leisure, luxury and license. They have been working to produce unbelievable material devices they believe would convert this world into a glorified heaven. Ignoring the stark reality of conditions described just above, that is!

Aldous Huxley said, "Most prophecy tends to oscillate between an extreme of gloom and the wildest optimism! The world, according to one set of seers, is headed for disaster; according to the other, the world is destined—within a generation or two—to become a kind of gigantic Disneyland, in which the human race will find perpetual happiness playing with an endless assortment of ever more ingenious mechanical toys."

How true. And also how ironic, that those voicing the

most glamorous predictions of science and industry seem to totally exclude the stark reality of world conditions—and, for that matter, seem unable to comprehend the additional snarls and problems their own predictions would bring.

However, leaving the facts aside, let us take a look at some of the speculations for our future.

In his book, *The Next 200 Years* (1976), futurist Herman Kahn—Director of the Hudson Institute "think tank" in New York—suggests that the world economy will continue to grow well into the next century, bringing a growing standard of living and increasing affluence to the majority of the world's population. He paints a picture of a prosperous global utopia by the year 2176, brought about by continuing technology advances—with plenty of energy, food and raw materials for all.

"Two hundred years from now, we believe, people almost everywhere will be rich, numerous and in control of the forces of nature," Kahn predicts. In his scenario, the world two centuries from now will contain some 15 billion people, with a staggering per-capita income of some $20,000, compared with only about $1,300 today.

In a previous study focusing on life in the United States in the years to A.D. 2000, Kahn forecasts a glittering utopia coming a great deal sooner than the world at large. He predicted that in the years just ahead, Americans would be enjoying "three-day weekends, three- or four-month vacations, Southern California-type living with the emphasis on family and home, high income, an abundance of material things. . . . " He asserted that people will live in ten-room houses, earn a disposable income (after taxes) of multiple tens of thousands of dollars, and enjoy a four-hour work day, five days per week—or maybe even a six-hour work day and a three-day week, with a four-day weekend.

5

In essence, we are to look forward to a life of almost complete idleness and leisure—the "good life" day after day after day. In short, a perpetual vacation!

But Is This Utopia?

But does this kind of a society sound truly good to you?

Think about these glowing predictions. Then think of the utter impracticability, and of the many problems they would create, rather than solve. Yet multiple millions, especially in the United States, anticipate such developments, hopefully in their own lifetimes, while turning a blind eye to the ominous warnings by other respected scientists who see instead impending doom for large segments of the world through famine, pestilence and war.

Can a tiny segment of the population of one nation expect to succeed in achieving ever more dizzying heights of material wealth, playing with an ever more dazzling assortment of mechanical gadgets, and ignore the awesome problems of the rest of the world?

Reporting on the paradoxes posed by the projected advancements in store for future society, a science writer of a leading newspaper asked a few years ago "What sort of world in 20 years?"

The answers were interesting.

He first told of new knowledge in biological science applied to medicine, giving new insight into, and partial control of, aging, heredity, mental illness, heart disease, cancer and virus infections.

Whole hosts of ingenious devices in the fields of applied physics and advanced engineering would provide super-sophisticated computers, communication satellites, novel transportation techniques, space exploration probes, and a newer and more glittering array of medical instruments and techniques.

He envisioned bigger crowds at bigger stadiums watching bigger athletic contests. Recreation, physical pleasure, fun, would be widespread. More golf courses, more swimming pools, tennis courts, dance halls, bowling alleys, color television sets—these were predicted to aid society in seeking ever more heightened pleasures.

But, he said, the years ahead "will have increased crime, gambling, sexual promiscuity, riots, air and water pollution, traffic congestion, noise, and lack of solitude." "More and more," continued the prediction, "there will be 'no place to hide.' "

Even Dr. Kahn, in his study of the United States of the future, admits that the "utopian" changes in lifestyles and work patterns could carry with them some traumatic consequences. "Many," he explains, will be satisfied but others will find such a life meaningless and purposeless, and they will look for something to fulfill them. Kahn suggests that we may see more riots and irrational movements, along with a turn to mysticism, cults and drugs as a means for such fulfillment.

We have seen an upsurge in drug usage, with certain drugs—notably marijuana and cocaine—becoming increasingly accepted by large numbers seeking escape from modern society, with the use of the latest popular drug, "angel dust," (phencyclidine, also called PCP), becoming a crisis of epidemic proportions in the U.S., according to police and hospital officials.

Accidents, suicides, homicides—all have been the end result of using angel dust. Yet multiple thousands continue to "find reality" through its use.

After drugs . . . then what? What other forms of escapism would the supposedly affluent, leisurely utopian life

7

of tomorrow bring with it, assuming it comes about at all?

Reading such reports of the "bad news," as well as the "good news," we may well have doubts about whether we want to be around in such an age.

Would We Really Want It?

But how about looking at society in general?

The same report adds that, because of intensified social, ethnic and racial problems, the cities of the future will be "seething centers of periodically great turmoil and confusion.

"For the underdeveloped world . . . , the 'plight of the average man' will have deteriorated. People will be more poorly fed and there will be fewer goods per person. Every attempt to improve the situation will be wiped out by the continued population growth. Hunger, starvation and famine periodically and continuously will stalk major portions of the planet. . . . "

Then, almost incredibly, the report said probably "for the first time in history, every child everywhere will be at school—if they are not starving in a famine"(!).

And so go the paradoxical and often conflicting prognostications of science, industry, and technology.

Not very happy predictions, are they?

Other prognostications abound, even about our personal futures. Some include:

Choosing the sex of children before they are conceived—1980.

Artificial plastic and electronic organs for humans—1982. (Wouldn't you far rather avoid getting sick, and keep healthy organs of your own?)

Artificial heart implantations; brain linked to computer—1985.

8

Chemical synthesis of inexpensive, nutritious food; cancer conquered—1990.

First human clone; brain transplants commonplace—1995.

Transplantation of almost all organs of the body—2000.

Alteration of the processes of aging—2005.

Biochemicals to aid the growth of new organs and limbs—2007.

Widespread use of artificial insemination to produce genetically superior offspring—2010.

Drugs to raise the level of intelligence—2012.

Fetuses grown in artificial wombs—2015.

Genetic engineering in humans by chemically modifying their DNA chains; human brain linked with computer to enlarge man's intellect—2020.

Total mastery of human genetics and heredity—2030.

Suspended animation of life—2040.

Complete control of the aging process; man-made immortality—2050.

The above prognostications were adapted in part from *The Post-Physician Era: Medicine in the 21st Century,* by Jerrold Maxmen (1976).

The predictions are almost endless. Economists, sociologists, geneticists, psychiatrists, even zoologists and anthropologists, are having a hand at predicting the varicolored and kaleidoscopic never-never land of tomorrow—glittering and glamorous for the few; filled with grisly spectres of horror for the many.

It Won't Happen

So there you have the two opposite, divergent views of scientists, statesmen, educators, world leaders—one glowingly optimistic about the progress of society; the other utterly hopeless.

But both of these concepts are false!

Man wants desperately to save the society he has established upon this earth. But this society—this civilization can't be saved! Man, himself, is bringing this world to destruction. God Almighty will soon step in, and create a new, peaceful, and happy society—the world *tomorrow*.

2

One Last "Obituary" Look at Today's World

BEFORE WE LOOK AT WHAT AC-
tually is going to come—the peaceful,
happy, joyful world tomorrow—let's
take one last "obituary" look at this world man has built
upon the earth. Take one last look at the corpses of education, science, technology, commerce and industry, governments, the social order, and religion.

Of course many see only the glitter, glamour, and tinsel
of today's world and think it is good. They see the temporary
pleasures, blind their eyes to the hard cold facts of reality.
Others, more aware of the world they live in, seek escape to
remote, unspoiled areas, where they can start anew, "away
from it all," and in harmony with the ecology. However,
there isn't really anywhere to go—remember the man who,

before World War II started, thought the safest place to be was Guadalcanal?

Education Is Decadent

But take a realistic look at this world's civilization.

We look at modern education first, because it is the mother—the alma mater—which has spawned the scientists, captains of industry and business, the politicians and rulers, the leaders in the modern social order, and the theologians.

Today's world is what its leaders have made it. And the leaders are the product of modern education. Education is defined by the *Encyclopaedia Britannica* as a system by which adult leaders of a society inject their philosophies, ideas, customs and culture into the minds of the growing generation. Education is, and has been through the centuries, essentially pagan in origin and character. The academic system was founded by the pagan philosopher Plato.

The 19th and 20th centuries have witnessed the absorption of German rationalism into the educational bloodstream—an approach that regards human reason as the chief source and test of knowledge. There has been a dangerous drift into materialism and collectivism. God is ignored. Revelation is rejected. The ancient belief of gnosticism, meaning *we know*, was succeeded by agnosticism, meaning *we don't know* (we are ignorant!). This ignorance is glorified as knowledge. Professing themselves to be wise, have not the educated become fools? Compare this with Romans 1:22 in the Bible.

Modern education trains students to earn a living in the professions, occupations and vocations—but fails to teach them how to live! It commits the crime of developing the machine, but it fails to develop the man.

In modern education we find perpetuation of false val-

12

ues, the teaching of distorted history, warped psychology, perverted arts and sciences, worthless knowledge.

Recently a leading expert on educational philosophy, Dr. Donald M. Dozer (professor emeritus of history at the university of California at Santa Barbara), in an article entitled "Educational Humbuggery," wrote this about contemporary university education:

"Ours is an age dominated by half-truths, and for this situation many causes can be found, not the least of which are attributable to the processes of higher education.

"American universities," he added, "have succumbed to the cult of faddism, sensationalism, and even vulgarism. New courses in scatology, whether masquerading as sociology, anthropology, or literature, have been given classroom platforms and respectability. . . . As students have become increasingly involved in curricular planning they have encouraged the idea that courses rich in content inhibit their creative impulses and represent an imposition upon them. This has led to the multiplication of colleges of creative studies, which might better be called colleges of undisciplined studies where lectures are eschewed as 'bourgeois' and students educate themselves in 'rap' sessions" (*The University Bookman,* winter, 1978).

A tree is known by its fruits. A mixed-up, unhappy and fearful world in chaos, divided against itself, filled with heartaches, frustrations, broken homes, juvenile delinquency, crime, insanity, racial hatreds, riots and violence, wars and death; devoid of honesty, truth and justice; now facing extinction by man-inflicted cosmocide—that is the fruit of modern education.

This materialistic knowledge God calls foolishness— *For the wisdom of this world is foolishness with God . . .* (I Cor. 3:19)

13

So what's the cause of this educated foolishness? This day of man—from creation of the human race to Christ's coming back to rule—has been a period of 6,000 years during which God *sentenced* the human world—except for those specially called of God—to being cut off from God and His revealed knowledge. Human knowledge without the Holy Spirit of God has been confined to the physical and material.

The first man, Adam, having the opportunity to make a choice between being thus limited in knowledge, or yielding to God's government (and hence receiving God's Holy Spirit), chose the former. Actually, the natural human mind, with only the human spirit (discussed under explanation of human nature later), is only half complete. Man needs God's Spirit as well as the human spirit given from birth.

Yes, today's educational intellectualism is ready to die. It will be replaced by the right and true educational system of the world tomorrow. This new-day system already has been introduced, and, like the proverbial grain of mustard seed, already is beginning to spread around the world— teaching young men and women the true values; the purpose of human life; the way to peace, prosperity, happiness, abundant living. All this is made possible only through the Holy Spirit, providing *spiritual comprehension*. In the world tomorrow this true education will banish illiteracy, and cover the earth as the ocean beds are covered with water!

Science and Technology

Today's world looks with awe at modern science as the messiah trusted to deliver it from poverty, ignorance, disease and unhappiness—to solve all its problems.

Science and technology, teamed with commerce and industry, promise the magic, push-button dream world of leisure, luxury and license.

But modern science has failed utterly to reveal to the world the purpose of human life or explain its true meaning. It remains ignorant of the true values. It does not know the *way* to peace! It has failed miserably to deliver the world from poverty, famine, disease, fears and worries, unhappiness. It has not rid the world of broken homes, crime, insanity, immorality.

A realistic look at the fruits of modern science leads only to disillusionment. Science and technology confine their attention to the realm of the material and the mechanical. Purpose and meaning of human life? The true values? Finding the *way* to peace, happiness and joy? We find these basics to human welfare are not their concern! These essentials are outside their field.

Look again to their fruits. True enough, we find the accelerating invention and production of intricate mechanical devices, labor-saving mechanisms that inspire admiration, and spectacular entertainment and amusement devices.

But, then, we also observe that people have not been taught to put added hours, days, and weeks of leisure to beneficial uses. The fruit here is increasing idleness, aversion to work, covetousness, desire for more and more—and dissatisfaction with it when it is acquired! These turn out, in practical application, to be false values, which only increase unhappiness.

Also we find an increasing segment of adolescents, who, with money to spend and nothing but idleness on their hands, become frustrated, staring a hopeless future in the face, turning to immorality, drugs, violence, and—too often—suicide!

And, after all, the principal contribution of modern science and technology has been the production of constantly

15

more terrifying weapons of mass destruction. Push-button world? Yes, today either of two men could push a button, and destroy two whole continents, probably culminating in the total extinction of mankind.

Modern science stands exposed as a false messiah—the Frankenstein monster threatening to destroy the mankind that created it.

Commerce and Industry

Turning to the realms of commerce and industry, surely, *here*, we find a spectacle of development that excites our enraptured admiration. Here we find an astonishing condition that would cause people who lived a century ago—could they suddenly come back to life—to gasp in amazed wonderment.

The telephone, radio, television, the motion picture in full color, the motor car, hundred-mile-an-hour railroad trains, mammoth oil-tankers, jet planes, spacecraft hurtling astronauts around the earth in outer space in 90 minutes, and that send men to the moon and back, unmanned spacecraft that take close-up photographs of the surfaces of Mars and Jupiter, the gadgets and modern electrical devices, the incredible modern computers—just to name a few.

Commerce and industry each is a world within a world—a fast-moving, pulsating world of high-geared activity. Surely all these magic productions cannot be bad? No—but most of them are being made to serve bad purposes, as well as good.

And, if we look further, we find these vibrant, high-pressure fields of activity based on competition and greed, appealing too often, in marketing their products, to vanity and wrong desires, utilizing dishonesty, misrepresentation, deception, unfair dealing. The motivating incentive is to give less, while charging more!

"Is honesty the best policy?" A magazine survey some years back put this question to 103 business executives—all high in their fields. An overwhelming majority doubted whether a strictly honest policy would enable a man to rise to the top in the business world. Only two answered "Yes," and one of these said he knew he was being naive.

Said one: "People who don't get dirty don't make it."

"In thirty years," said another, "I've known of only three men who've reached executive positions cleanly, and I admit I'm not one of them."

"The higher the executive is in the management ladder," said a third, "the more likely he is to do some dirty work."

An appraisal of the field of modern business reveals selfish motivation, disregard for public good, sharp practices, dishonesty, dog-eat-dog competition! We emphatically do not find here the true values and the outgoing concern for others that would give happiness to the world.

The Field of Government

The politicians in the field of government are said to be in public service. They profess to be "public servants." They are installed in offices of authority and power. They execute the laws that regulate and govern the people. Theirs is the power to regulate society, guide it, and make it what it is. They are the leaders of the people.

When we turn the searchlight on government in today's modern world, we meet it, once again, with sad and discouraging disillusionment. Today, as of old in ancient times, too many of those who seek offices of power over the people of cities, states, districts, or nations, promise great benefits, pose as public benefactors, while their inner motives are ambitions for personal power and wealth.

17

The modern world has produced three more-or-less new forms of government. Each promises peace, happiness, and prosperity for its people. They are: 1) French and United States republics; 2) Swedish- and British-type limited monarchy; 3) atheistic communism.

All three are based on a system of industry, and on diffusion of education, and all three are predicated on the theory that every individual has the right to share in the benefits of science, industry, and the modern life.

But actually too often what we find is selfish, greedy men of excessive vanity, ambitious in their lust for rule, scheming to get their hands on the throttle of power for personal aggrandizement and monetary gain. We find secret deals, graft, immorality, deception, dishonesty, running rampant in high places.

Governments promise peace—but bring wars. They promise benefits for the people, and then extract from the people the cost of the benefits plus excessive costs of government. Government promises are empty. The people are the pawns who fork over the money, in order to get a part of it back. We fail to find in human government any knowledge of life's purpose, or dissemination of the true values.

The Social Order

What about civilization? Let someone suggest a possible stupendous worldwide calamity that might destroy civilization.

People would exclaim, horrified, "What? Destroy civilization?" as if that would mean the destruction and ending of everything worthwhile—everything people have to live for.

People think of civilization as the sum-total of everything good that mankind has struggled from the dawn of

18

history to establish. People think of civilization as the far-advanced, intelligent, well-ordered human society that is good to the point of perfection. The acme of human progress! Perhaps *you* have accepted this popular assumption.

But is this world's civilization really good?

If the facets of human life and organization so far examined have brought disillusionment, surely, we would think, the social order ought to be good—evidencing great human progress—a proud monument to human advancement. So now we look behind the scenes. Now we turn the searchlight of truth on the social order of civilization.

We look first at the most populous nations, where far more than half the world's population lives—China, the countries of Southeast Asia and Indonesia, India, the Arab countries of the Middle East, and most of Africa—as well as much of South America. And what do we see here? Illiteracy, ignorance, retrogression, famine, disease; people living in unbelievable poverty, filth, squalor, stench beyond description. Victims of famine and widespread epidemics of disease—in many places half of all babies die during their first year of life. Wretched beings, ill-housed, ill-fed, ill-clothed.

Is that part—the biggest part—of this world's humanity an example of progress, and a culture worth preserving?

But now focus the floodlight of truth on the affluent "have" nations. Do we find the social order of the Western world based on understanding of life's purpose and true meaning, pursuing the true values that produce universal happiness?

Regretfully, quite the contrary. In purely social functions and contacts—especially among the elite of high society—we find an unhappy competition in snobbery and vanity, with class distinctions, racial discrimination, religious bigotry, selfish motives.

Look at amusements and recreations. The prevailing format in motion pictures and television is illicit sex, violence, and murder. Young twelve- to fifteen-year-olds hear the beat and see the wiggle, and give themselves over in a virtually possessed frenzy to rock music. Children start going steady about age twelve or thirteen, and a theologian-labeled new morality becomes "understanding" about premarital sex, adultery and perversion.

Juveniles stare in the face a hopeless future, descend into delinquency, and in rebellion against society, organize into gangs.

One in ten today is mentally sick. Crime and violence are on the upsurge. Divorce stalks the Western world (one for every three marriages,) leaving broken homes and frustrations in its wake. Even those who mount the ladder of success—the millionaires—relentlessly seek more millions; and are never satisfied with what they acquire when they have it.

This world's civilization is mentally, morally and spiritually sick! It supplies no purpose for life, knows nothing of the true values, has no concept of the right meaning of the word "success."

This world's civilization has been making progress in reverse. It has become decadent, putrid, rotten, filthy, and is now bringing about its own destruction!

But the future is not hopeless. This present evil world is to be replaced—in our time—by the happy, joyous, peaceful world tomorrow.

What Has Religion Contributed?

Well, surely we should expect to find, at long last, in religion the knowledge of life's purpose, the true values, and

20

the right ways that should make this world a better world—a happy world—a peaceful world.

Here, at last, we must surely find a stabilizing and uplifting influence for society.

Yet, shocking though it be—incredible though it is—if we put the searchlight on the facts, and view them realistically with an open mind, we find here the most sickening disillusionment of all.

Reluctant though we are to recognize it, we find the established religious organizations which profess the name of Jesus Christ teaching the diametric opposite of His teachings—condemning the customs He practiced—following, instead, the pagan customs He condemned!

The churches of the Western world are divided and in confusion. They have not converted, saved, and reformed the whole world as they profess to have been commissioned to do. If that be their mission, they have failed miserably.

Methodist Bishop Hazen G. Werner once said: "We have been dried out by the hot winds of secularism. We who are to overcome the world have been overcome by the world."

"The Church," said Harvard Divinity School's Dean Miller, "simply does not have a cutting edge [it has thrown away the 'two-edged sword'—the Bible]. It has taken the culture of our time and absorbed it."

To this, Yale's Chaplain Coffin agrees, "We churchmen are gifted at changing wine into water—watering down religion."

This world's so-called Christianity has taken the name of Christ—has proclaimed to the world that Jesus of Nazareth was the Christ—has preached the name of Christ with a Message about His Person—but they have rejected His Gospel—the Gospel God sent for all mankind by Him—the Gospel He taught.

21

Look at the other religions of the world—Buddhism, Shintoism, Taoism, Confucianism, Moslemism, Hinduism, and the others. In most countries where these religions are embraced, we find illiteracy, poverty, degeneration, misery, suffering, despair—general unhappiness. None of them has produced a happy world. They have spawned communal wars, hatreds, and violence.

Where, Now!

So we have appraised the major facets of modern civilization—this world's education, its science and technology, its commerce and industry, its systems of government, its social order, and its religions—the civilization man has developed, swayed by Satan. And we have found them all wrong—all evil—all decadent. They are ready to die. The 6,000 years of man is ending. But the Eternal God will soon usher in the utopian world of peace and happiness!

And where have these major branches of civilization brought us? Just what is the status of 20th Century "progress"? What is the actual state of the world today?

Just this.

When we take a hard, cold, realistic view of conditions and trends, they do point inevitably to a fast-approaching world crisis of combined nuclear war, starvation, uncontrollable disease epidemics, crime and violence, and the extinction of human life on this planet.

Man has no solution!

The farther he goes, the more destructive are his efforts.

And yet—absolute utopia is soon to grip this earth in our time, and we shall see world peace. We shall see sickness banished; vigorous health restored; ignorance replaced with universal right education; poverty replaced with universal prosperity; weeping and wailing turned into happiness and joy!

Incredible?

Why should it be?

Why?—yes, why should we have a world where more than half of the world's people are living in abject ignorance and poverty, wracked with disease and pain, living in filth and squalor and wretchedness? Why, even in our prosperous Western nations, should our lands be filled with sickness and pain; plagued by crime, violence, riots; broken and unhappy homes, juvenile delinquents of delinquent parents, frustrations with no hope for the future?

Why?

Does it make sense?

Do we not realize that there is a cause for every effect? Why are people blind to the cause of all this degeneration?

The Two Alternatives

Let's face it. Right now there are two alternatives. Either there does exist a living God of Supreme mind and total power, who very soon will step in and intervene in the affairs of this world, and save humanity from itself, or else the threatened extinction pictured above must inevitably soon occur.

There is no other alternative.

One may blind his eyes to existing facts, and trends, and say, "Now, come on! I can't see that this world is any worse than it ever was—nothing's going to happen. If we just ignore the conditions and don't worry, perhaps they'll just go away." But these conditions and trends won't just go away. Not unless they are caused to go away!

The Scriptures of the Holy Bible, the inspired revelation of that Supreme God to mankind, have foretold today's

23

world conditions and trends—and give us the advance news of coming peace on earth—of universal prosperity—of happiness and joy—of veritable utopia!

This is the good news of the world tomorrow.

And it is absolutely sure. It is sure, because it does not depend on men, or anything men might do. God is going to do it, in spite of rebellious man. Man would fail. Man always did fail. God never fails!

3

The Cause of All World Troubles

YOU LOOK AT TODAY'S NEWSPAPERS, and what do you see? War news. Crime is on the increase. Murder is commonplace. Terrible accidents. Riots break out in many nations, with many killed, etc.

Now let's take a look into the newspaper headlines of the near future, of the new world tomorrow that is going to come in our time.

And remember, it won't become utopia all at once. (That will be explained later.)

Take a Glimpse into Tomorrow

When the Supreme Ruler, Jesus Christ, comes again to earth already crowned as King of kings, in all the vast power and glory of Almighty God, the Gentile nations actually will resist Him at first. But He is coming to rule by divine force! What a travesty that the nations will have to be forced to be happy, prosperous, physically fit and well, living abundantly and joyfully.

But these might be the headlines you will read in the newspaper of the future:

"Crime Rate Drops to Zero."

"No Wars During This Year. Former Soldiers Being Rapidly Assimilated into Food Production and New Industries."

"Disease Epidemics Disappear. Millions Have Been Supernaturally Healed of Sickness and Disease. All Vaccines and 'Shots' Banned. Causes of Cancer, Heart Attacks, Other Fatal Diseases Revealed. Authorities Predict All Such Diseases to Disappear, by Avoiding Causes, Within Coming Year."

"Thousands of Hospital Properties Up for Sale. Sensational Decline in Sickness and Disease Releases Increasing Hundreds of Thousands of Doctors, Nurses, Attendants and Staff Personnel for Happier and More Useful Occupations. Knowledge of Causes Reduces Sickness and Disease. Thousands of Afflicted Now Being Divinely Healed."

"Rapid Increase in Food Production. All Records Broken for Increased Food Production. Agricultural Authorities Reveal Abolition of Artificial and Synthetic Fertilizers, and Return to Nature's Laws of Soil Enrichment Resulting Not Only in Bumper Crops, but Vastly Improved Quality and Flavor."

Well, how are those, for a starter?

We repeat, there's a cause for every effect.

If crime is to be greatly reduced, then wiped out, there will be a reason. People may have many guesses, opinions, theories about what causes crime, but the answer is, human nature.

26

What is the cause of wars? The answer is—human nature. Why do people steal, murder, commit adultery or fornication, covet what is not theirs? Human nature.

We shall never have Utopia on earth until human nature is changed. But, you say—"Man can't change human nature." Oh, But God can!

And that's precisely what the living Christ is going to do, when He returns to rule all the nations of the earth.

But What Is Human Nature?

We think customarily, don't we, that human nature is something with which humans are born.

But wait a moment. Stop and think. If there be a Creator God, did He design and create within humanity this thing we call human nature? Or, if one accepts the theory of evolution, did man inherit it from a lower species of vertebrates from which he is supposed to have evolved? There are both tame and wild animals. But take, for example, a cow, a dog, or an ape. They have instincts not hereditary in man. But human nature? Just what is human nature?

I define it as vanity, lust and greed toward self—and as jealousy, envy, hostility and resentment of authority against others. The Bible defines it thus: *The heart is deceitful above all things, and desperately wicked. . . .* (Jer. 17:9)—and *. . . the carnal* [natural] *mind is enmity* [hostile] *against God; for it is not subject to the law of God, neither indeed can be* (Rom. 8:7).

You cannot ascribe that attitude or nature to the dumb animals. Does it make sense to suppose a God of love, mercy and great outgoing concern for His human family, deliberately created us to be naturally hostile toward our Maker—not subject to His law, deceitful and desperately wicked?

27

Satan Not Created with It

Look at the biblical account of human creation. Before Satan got to Adam, God brought to Adam *every beast of the field, and every fowl of the air* (Gen. 2:19), asking Adam to give them names. Did Adam rebel? Did he say, "Go do it yourself?" Did Adam refuse to obey God's command? The answer: *And Adam gave names to all cattle, and to the fowl of the air, and to every beast of the field . . .* (verse 20). Adam at once did as God instructed.

But from Genesis 3, all through the Bible to Revelation 20, much is said repeatedly about Satan. Isaiah 14 identifies him as the former archangel Lucifer. And Ezekiel 28 affirms that he was a created super being, perfect in all his ways until by his own free choice, iniquity was found in him.

The former Lucifer turned to rebellion against God, to deceit, hostility, becoming cunning, subtle and desperately wicked. He came to be filled with vanity, lust and greed. He turned from God's way of love—which is outflowing concern and desire to help and share, the way of giving—to the way of getting.

Only Two Basic Philosophies

There are only two ways, or attitudes of life, broadly speaking: give, the way of love; and get, the way of vanity, selfishness, hostility, resentment.

The first man Adam, after Satan got to him through his wife, had turned to the way of get.

But we did not inherit that get way of life at birth from Adam. Adam was not created with it—he acquired it from Satan. And acquired characteristics are not passed on by heredity. Those who are called by God, and come to real repentance and belief in Christ, become partakers of—or

28

acquire—the Divine nature (II Pet. 1:4). But the children of one who has acquired it will not receive by heredity that divine nature.

Adam and Eve, by making the wrong decision, acquired the get attitude from Satan. All their children—the entire human family, with the single exception of Jesus Christ—have acquired it, after birth, from Satan.

How, you may ask, can that be?

Satan was still around when Jesus was born. Satan tried to have the Christ-child killed. He tempted Christ—unsuccessfully.

Satan was still around when the Apostle Paul wrote his inspired second letter to the Church at Corinth. . . . *I fear,* he wrote, *lest by any means as the serpent beguiled Eve through his subtilty, so your minds should be corrupted . . .* (II Cor. 11:3).

Those in the Corinthian Church were not born with this corruption of mind—they were in danger of acquiring it.

Satan Broadcasts!

It is explained in Ephesians 2:2: *Wherein in time past ye walked according to the prince of the power of the air, the spirit that now worketh in the children of disobedience.* Satan is a spirit being—and a very super one. He is prince of the "power of the air." He "broadcasts." Through the air! How does he, then, work in humans?

When God wanted to put it into the mind of King Cyrus of Persia to issue a proclamation to send a contingent of Jews back to Jerusalem to build the second temple, He *stirred up the spirit of Cyrus king of Persia* to do this (Ezra 1:1).

Every human has, from birth, not "human nature" but

a spirit (in the form of essence—not a "soul" or ghost), which imparts the power of intellect to the human brain. This human spirit cannot see. The physical brain sees through the eyes. Knowledge enters the brain through the senses of hearing, tasting, smelling, feeling. But the brain cannot see, hear, smell, taste or feel spirit. It is confined to physical, material knowledge.

Yet what knowledge enters the physical brain through these five senses is automatically "programmed" as in a computer—recorded in memory into this human spirit. This spirit in man, therefore, acts as a computer. It gives instant recall of knowledge stored in it to the brain. The brain utilizes this instant recall in the process of thinking, reasoning, decision-making.

The human spirit does not think—it empowers the physical brain to think. This human spirit does not supply human life. The human life is supplied by the physical breath of air, and by physical blood.

Yet, just as the spirit of ancient King Cyrus was utilized by God as a medium through which to transmit the thought into Cyrus's mind to issue the decree, so Satan transmits through the air—broadcasts—attitudes, impulses, desires of vanity, lust and greed, jealousy and envy, competition, rebellion against authority.

You Are on Satan's Wavelength

The spirit in each human is automatically tuned in on Satan's wavelength. Even after one is converted. So was Jesus' human spirit open to Satan's wavelength—but Jesus also, through the Holy Spirit, was in tune with God. Jesus therefore instantly rejected every temptation to vanity, selfishness, hostility toward God. So may, and should, the converted Christian.

30

Satan has no power of duress. He cannot force any human mind to submit to the attitude he broadcasts and attempts to instill. Every human is a free moral agent, responsible for his own attitudes, decisions and actions. Satan does not broadcast in words—merely in attitudes. If the human mind is willing, it will accept and yield to Satan's attitudes—attitudes we have mistakenly called "human nature"!

The human mind is *not* born with Satan's hostile, self-centered attitudes. Neither is a human born with the Divine nature which the thoroughly converted Christian may acquire. Yet as soon as an infant or little child begins to exercise his brain in the thinking process, Satan's broadcasts of the self-centered attitude begin reaching his brain through his human spirit. Jesus, and He only, had the Holy Spirit in full measure from human birth. Yet even He was tempted in all points as are we all—yet without ever yielding (Heb. 4:15).

Since the normal child mind begins receiving these impulses to accept Satan's attitudes very early in childhood, unless counteracted by parental teaching and influence he will automatically begin accepting these carnal attitudes. They became habitual—by habit they are acquired as a nature. But, just as the converted human may acquire—become partaker of—the divine nature (II Pet. 1:4), so off-guard humans acquire and exhibit what we call "human nature"!

How God Will Change Human Nature

I have said that we shall never have real utopia on earth until human nature is changed, and that human nature is the villain cause of all this world's evils. And I also said that although man can't change his human nature, God can—

31

and will. That is precisely what the glorified world-ruling Christ is going to do when He returns to earth in Divine power and glory.

Now we can begin to understand.

First, consider how the living Christ, as our High Priest, changes this human nature in those whom God calls to salvation in this present day of man.

Each individual is a free moral agent, and God won't change that prerogative! Each must be brought, of his own free will, to repentance and to faith in Jesus Christ. Those are the conditions. Those do not change human nature. They are the conditions God requires of us. But when we, of our own free choice, do yield to those two conditions, then God starts the changing process.

God doesn't abolish human nature—not as long as we are in the human flesh. But He does, upon real repentance and faith, give the precious gift of His Holy Spirit, which enters into the mind of the individual. And this is the Divine Nature. It is not human nature—it is God's Nature. Yet it does not drive out or eliminate human nature. Satan is still broadcasting—if you will listen.

But if one has really repented, and fully believes, he will want to be willingly led by God's Spirit. And it is *as many as are led by the Spirit of God that are the sons of God* (Romans 8:14). If one makes the decision to be led by this new Divine Nature, God's Spirit in him is also the power of God and the faith of Christ that will enable him to resist his human nature, and follow the Divine Nature. As the converted individual resists the pulls of human nature, and is led by God's Holy Spirit into obedience to God's ways, he grows in spiritual character, until at the time of the Resurrection, his human nature will be gone—only the Divine nature will remain.

How Utopia Will Come!

But now let's be specific.

Let's see just how tomorrow's Utopia is to be ushered in. Remember, this wonderful world-state will not be achieved all at once.

Every major step of these soon-coming events is laid bare before our eyes in Biblical prophecy.

The same Jesus Christ who walked over the hills and valleys of the Holy Land and the streets of Jerusalem, more than 1,900 years ago is coming again. He said He would come again. After He was crucified, God raised Him from the dead after three days and three nights (Matthew 12:40; Acts 2:32; I Corinthians 15:3-4). He ascended to the Throne of God, Headquarters of the Government of the Universe (Acts 1:9-11; Hebrews 1:3; 8:1; 10:12; Revelation 3:21).

He is the *nobleman* of the parable, who went to the Throne of God—the *far country*—to be coronated as King of kings over all nations, and then to return to earth (Luke 19:11-27).

Again, He is in heaven until the *times of restitution of all things* (Acts 3:19-21). *Restitution* means restoring to a former state or condition. In this case, the restoring of God's Government on earth, and thus, the restoring of world peace, and utopian conditions.

Present world turmoil, escalating wars and contentions will climax in world trouble so great that, unless God intervenes, no human flesh would be *saved* alive (Matthew 24:22). At its very climax when delay would result in blasting all life from off this planet, Jesus Christ will return. This time He is coming as Divine God. He is coming in all the power and glory of the Universe-Ruling Creator. (Matthew

33

24:30; 25:31.) He is coming as *King of kings and Lord of lords* (Revelation 19:16), to establish world super-government and rule all nations *with a rod of iron* (Revelation 19:15; 12:5; Matthew 25:31-32).

Think of it. The glorified Christ—coming in all the splendor, the supernatural power and the glory of God Almighty—coming to save mankind alive—coming to stop escalating wars, nuclear mass destruction, human pain and suffering—coming to usher in peace, abundant well-being, happiness and joy for all mankind. But will He be welcomed by the nations?

World famous scientists now say frankly that the *only* hope for survival on earth is a supreme world-ruling government, controlling all military power. They admit that is impossible for man to accomplish. Christ is coming to give us just that.

But will He be welcome?

A leading American newsweekly gave the following surprising appraisal of man's *only hope:* The once optimistic hope of Americans, the article said, for a well-ordered and stable world, is fading. Expenditures close to a trillion dollars have failed to provide stability. Rather conditions have worsened. This appraisal indicated that among officials, the prevailing view is gaining acceptance that tensions and world problems are becoming too deep-seated to be solved "except by a strong hand from someplace."

"A strong hand from someplace." God Almighty is going to send a very strong hand from "someplace" to save humanity!

Christ Unwelcome?

But will humanity shout with joy, and welcome Him in frenzied ecstasy and enthusiasm?

34

They will not! They will believe, because the false ministers of Satan (II Corinthians 11:13-15) have deceived them, that He is the Anti-Christ. The nations will be angry at His coming (Revelation 11:15 with 11:18), and the military forces will actually attempt to fight Him to destroy Him (Revelation 17:14).

The nations will be engaged in the climactic battle of the coming World War III, with the battlefront at Jerusalem (Zechariah 14:1-2) and then Christ will return. In supernatural power He will *fight against those nations* that fight against Him! (Verse 3.) He will totally defeat them! (Revelation 17:14.) *His feet shall stand in that day upon the Mount of Olives*, a very short distance to the east of Jerusalem (Zechariah 14:4).

How Nations Will Submit

When the glorified all-Powerful Christ first comes again to earth, the nations will be angry. The military forces gathered at Jerusalem will try to fight Him! I said "try." But far more powerful armies follow Christ from heaven—all the holy angels. (Revelation 19:14, identified in Matthew 25:31.)

Want to see a description of that battle—and what will happen to those hostile human armies?

In Revelation 17, the armies of the now-rising United States of Europe—the resurrected Roman Empire—are referred to in verses 13-14: *These shall make war with the Lamb* [Christ], *and the Lamb shall overcome them: for He is Lord of lords, and King of kings. . . .*

But how will He overcome them? We find that in the 14th chapter of Zechariah:

And this shall be the plague wherewith the [Eternal] *will smite all the people* [armies] *that have fought against*

Jerusalem; Their flesh shall consume away while they stand upon their feet, and their eyes shall consume away in their holes, and their tongue shall consume away in their mouth (Zechariah 14:12).

Perhaps it is even plainer in the Revised Standard Version: *And this shall be the plague with which the* [Eternal] *will smite all the people that wage war against Jerusalem: their flesh shall rot while they are still on their feet, their eyes shall rot in their sockets, and their tongues shall rot in their mouths.*

This rotting of their flesh off their bones will happen almost instantaneously—*while they are still on their feet.*

What a divine retribution against armies that will fight against Christ. What a demonstration of the Divine Power with which the glorified Christ will rule all nations. Rebellion against God's Law and God's rule must, and speedily will be put down.

Can you realize that every unhappiness, every evil that has come to humanity, has been the result of transgressing God's Law?

If no one ever had any other god before the true God, if all children were reared to honor, respect, and obey their parents, and all parents reared their children in God's Ways, if no one ever allowed the spirit of murder to enter his heart, if there were no wars, no killing of humans by humans, if all marriages were kept happy and there were no transgressions of chastity before or after marriage, if all had so much concern for the good and welfare of others that no one would steal—and we could throw away all locks, keys, and safes, if everyone told the truth—everyone's word were good—everyone were honest, if no one ever coveted what was not rightfully his, but had so much outgoing concern for the welfare of others

36

that he really believed it is more blessed to *give* than to receive—what a happy world we would have!

In such a world, with all loving and worshipping God with all their minds, hearts, and strength—with all having concern for the welfare of all others equal to concern for self—there would be no divorce—no broken homes or families, no juvenile delinquency, no crime, no jails or prisons, no police except for peaceful direction and supervision as a public service for all, no wars, no military establishments.

But, further, God has set in motion physical laws that operate in our bodies and minds, as well as the spiritual Law. There would be no sickness, ill health, pain or suffering. There would be, on the contrary, vigorous, vibrant good health, filled with dynamic interest in life, enthusiastic interest in constructive activities bringing happiness and joy. There would be cleanliness, vigorous activity, real progress, no slums, no degenerate backward races or areas of earth.

Resurrected Saints

As the resurrected Christ ascended to heaven in clouds, so He shall return to earth in clouds (Acts 1:9-11; Matthew 24:30). Just *as* He is returning (I Thessalonians 4:14-17), the dead in Christ—those who have received and been led by God's Holy Spirit (Romans 8:11, 14), will rise in a gigantic resurrection, made immortal—including all the prophets of old (Luke 13:28). Those who have the Spirit of God, then living, shall be instantaneously changed from mortal to immortal (I Corinthians 15:50-54) and, together with those resurrected, shall rise to meet the descending glorified Christ (I Thessalonians 4:17) in the clouds in the air. They shall be with Him, where He is, forever (John 14:3). They shall—with Him—come down out of the clouds, and stand with

37

Him, therefore, that very same day, on the Mount of Olives (Zechariah 14:4-5).

These changed, converted saints, now made immortal, will then rule the nations—nations of mortals—under Christ (Daniel 7:22; Revelation 2:26-27; 3:21).

Satan Removed At Last!

This most glorious event in all earth's history—the supernatural majestic descent to earth, in the clouds, of the glorified all-powerful Christ—will at long last put an end to the subtile, deceitful, invisible rule of Satan.

The coming of Christ in supreme glory as King of kings and Lord of lords is recorded in Revelation 19.

But in Revelation 20:1-3, the advance news is recorded: *And I saw an angel come down from heaven, having the key of the bottomless pit, and a great chain in his hand. And he laid hold on that old serpent, which is the Devil, and Satan, and bound him a thousand years, and cast him into the bottomless pit, and shut him up, and set a seal upon him, that he should deceive the nations no more, till the thousand years should be fulfilled: and after that, he must be loosed for a little season.*

The day of man, swayed, deceived, misled by Satan for 6,000 years, will be over.

No longer will Satan be able to broadcast through the air into the spirit in man. No longer shall he be able to inject into unsuspecting humans his satanic nature—which we have been misled into calling "human nature."

Human Nature Not to Disappear at Once

But that does not mean that the acquired satanic attitude will disappear from human minds immediately. The multiplied millions shall have acquired it. And even though

38

Satan will then be restrained from continuing to broadcast it, what has been acquired as habit will not be automatically removed.

Yet God has made us humans free moral agents. He has given us control over our own minds, except as we may be blinded by Satan's pull of evil by deception.

But no longer will earth's mortal humans be deceived. Now the all-Powerful Christ, and the immortal saints ruling under Him, will begin removing the scales that have blinded human minds.

That is why I say complete utopia cannot be ushered in all at once. Multiple millions will still hold to the attitude of rebellion—of vanity, lust and greed. But with Christ's coming shall begin the process of *re*-education—of opening deceived minds—of *un*deceiving minds, and bringing them to a voluntary repentance.

From the time of Christ's supernatural take over, and Satan's banishment, God's Law and the word of the Eternal shall go forth from Zion, spreading over the whole earth (Isa. 2:3).

The 6,000-year *sentence* God placed on Adam's world, of being cut off from God, will be ended. Christ will begin calling all mortals on earth to repentance and spiritual salvation! God's Holy Spirit shall flow out from Jerusalem (Zech. 14:8).

What glory! A new day shall have dawned. Peace shall soon come. Men shall turn from the way of "get" to the way of "give"—God's way of love.

A NEW CIVILIZATION shall now grip the earth!

4

The New World Government

NOW NOTICE JUST HOW THE NEW World Government will function! It will not be so-called Democracy. It will not be Socialism. It will not be Communism or Fascism. It will not be human monarchy, oligarchy, or plutocracy. It will not be man's government over man. Man has proven his utter incapability of ruling himself.

It will be Divine Government—the Government of God. It will not be government from the bottom up. The people will have no votes. It will not be government of or by the people—but it will be government for the people. It will be government from the top (God Almighty) down.

There will be no election campaigns. No campaign fund-raising dinners. No dirty political campaigns, where each candidate attempts to put himself forward in the most favorable light, defaming, denouncing, discrediting his opponents. No time will be wasted in mudslinging campaigns in the lust for power.

No human will be given any government office. All in government service will then be Divine Spirit beings, in the Kingdom of God—the God Family.

All officials will be appointed—and by the Divine Christ, who reads and knows men's hearts, their inner character, and abilities or lack of ability. You'll find a description of Christ's supernatural insight into the very character of others in Isaiah 11:1-5.

Notice it: *And the spirit of the* [Eternal] *shall rest upon him, the spirit of wisdom and understanding, the spirit of counsel and might, the spirit of knowledge and of the fear of the* [Eternal]; *and shall make him of quick understanding . . . and he shall not judge after the sight of his eyes, neither reprove after the hearing of his ears* [hearsay], *but with righteousness shall He judge the poor, and reprove with equity for the meek of the earth* (Isaiah 11:2-4).

Remember, God is the Supreme One who is love—who gives—who rules with outgoing concern for the ruled. He will rule for the highest good of the people. The most able, the most righteous, those best fitted for office will be placed in all offices of responsibility and power.

There will then be two kinds of beings on earth—humans, being ruled by those made divine.

Some resurrected saints will rule over ten *cities*, some over five (Luke 19:17-19).

Think of it—no money wasted on political campaigns. No splits in political parties with quarreling and hatreds. No political parties!

What Is the New Covenant?

In short, under the new Covenant which Christ is coming to usher in, what we shall see on earth is happiness,

41

peace, abundance, and justice for all. Did you ever read just what this New Covenant will consist of? Did you suppose it will do away with God's Law? Exactly the opposite. *For this is the covenant* that Christ is coming to establish, you'll read in Hebrews 8:10, *I will put my laws into their mind, and write them in their hearts. . . .*

When God's Laws are in our hearts—when we love God's ways, and in our hearts want to live by them, human nature will be put under subjection—people will want to live the Way that is the cause of peace, happiness, abundance, joyful well-being!

But remember—the humans remaining on the earth—after Christ's return, ruled then by Christ and those resurrected or changed to immortality—will themselves still have human nature. They will be still unconverted.

But Christ and the governing Kingdom of God, then set up as the Governing Family, will bring about the coming utopia by two basic courses of action.

Two Courses of Action

1) All crime, and organized rebellion will be put down by force—Divine supernatural force.

2) Christ will then set His hand to reeducate and to save or spiritually convert the world.

Notice, first, how the social and religious customs will be changed by Divine force.

Originally God gave seven annual Festivals and Holy Days He commanded to be observed. They contained great and important meaning. They pictured God's Master Plan for working out His purpose for humanity. They were established forever. Jesus observed them, setting us an example. The apostles observed them (Acts 18:21, 20:6, 16;

I Cor. 5:8, 16:8). The Church—including Gentile converts—kept them.

They were God's way—God's customs for His people. But people rejected God's ways and customs, and turned, instead, to the ways and customs of the pagan religions. People did what seemed right to themselves. These same wrong ways seem right to most people today! We realize they seem right—not wrong—to most who will be reading these words.

But can we realize that *there is a way which seemeth right unto a man, but the end thereof are the ways of death?* (Proverbs 14:12). And if you turn to Proverbs 16:25 you will see the same thing repeated: *There is a way that seemeth right unto a man, but the end thereof are the ways of death.*

God said through Moses: *Ye shall not do after all the things that we do here this day, every man whatsoever is right in his own eyes* (Deuteronomy 12:8). And again: *Take heed to thyself that thou be not snared by following them* [pagan religious customs] *. . . and that thou enquire not after their gods saying, How did these nations serve their gods? even so will I do likewise. Thou shalt not do so unto the* [Eternal] *thy God: for every abomination to the* [Eternal], *which he hateth, have they done unto their gods . . .* (Deuteronomy 12:30-31).

Today the professing Christian world rejects God's Holy Days; holy to Him, but which a deceived "Christianity" hates. They observe instead the pagan days—Christmas, New Year's, Easter, and others—"which God hateth"! Many know and confess that these are pagan—but they argue, "We don't observe these in worshipping the pagan gods, we use their customs in worshipping Christ and the true God."

That is the way that *seemeth right* to people. They may not mean any wrong. They are deceived. A deceived man doesn't know he is wrong. He thinks he is right. He may be as sincere as those who have found God's way and obey it. Yet God says He will not accept that kind of observance or worship. It is an abomination to Him—"which He hateth."

But it is those who have been deceived, whose eyes God will open to His truth, when Christ returns to rule all nations of mortals still left alive.

All Will Keep God's Festivals

People will no longer be blinded and deceived in regard to God's commands and ways. Then He will enforce obedience to His customs.

Go back to the 14th chapter of Zechariah:

And it shall come to pass, that every one that is left of all the nations which came against Jerusalem [that is, those who were not in the armies supernaturally destroyed] *shall even go up from year to year to worship the King, the* [Eternal] *of hosts, and to keep the feast of tabernacles* (verse 16).

This *feast of tabernacles* is one of the seven annual Festivals God commanded His people to observe. But ancient Israel rebelled. They rejected God's Festivals, and turned to pagan festivals. The Jewish people, after Ezra and Nehemiah, observed them. But false "Christian" ministers taught that God's Festivals were part of the old Mosaic system—not for us today. The clergy deceived and prejudiced the people. The people were deceived into believing that Christmas, New Year's, Easter, etc., were days Christ ordained.

But now Christ is returning to earth to restore God's ways—including God's Festivals. Those who rebelliously won't keep God's Holy Days now—who sneer at them in scathing contempt, will observe them when Christ returns. Notice what this scripture says:

And it shall be, that whoso will not come up of all the families of the earth [including Gentile nations] *unto Jerusalem to worship the King, the* [Eternal] *of hosts, even upon them shall be no rain. And if the family of Egypt go not up, and come not, that have no rain; there shall be the plague, wherewith the* [Eternal] *will smite the heathen that come not up to keep the feast of tabernacles. This shall be the punishment of Egypt, and the punishment of all nations that come not up to keep the feast of tabernacles* (Zechariah 14:17-19).

These passages give us the method by which Christ will *rule with a rod of iron*—of how He will use supernatural force to bring people of all nations to His right ways—ways that are the cause of real blessings.

The Perfect Government

Yes, Jesus Christ very soon is going to return to this earth. He is coming in power and glory. He is coming to *rule* all nations!

But He is not going to do this ruling, supervising, all alone, by Himself. He is coming to set up world government. It will be a highly organized government. There will be many positions of authority.

Right here, it is time we stop to explain the mechanics of this perfect form of government.

First, it is the government of God—not human government. Man won't acknowledge it yet, but man has demonstrated by 6,000 years of inefficient, bungling, wasteful efforts of human government that mortal man is utterly incapable of rightly governing himself.

As for man being qualified to rule and administer government, God says of government officials today: *None calleth for justice, nor any pleadeth for truth: they trust in vanity and speak lies; they conceive mischief, and bring forth*

45

iniquity. . . . Their feet run to evil, and they make haste to shed innocent blood: their thoughts are thoughts of iniquity; wasting and destruction are in their paths. The way of peace they know not; and there is no judgment in their goings: they have made them crooked paths: whosoever goeth therein shall not know peace.

Then the people, under this human *mis*-government, say: *Therefore is judgment far from us, neither doth justice overtake us: we wait for light* [solution of civil, personal, national, and world problems], *but behold obscurity; for brightness, but we walk in darkness. We grope for the wall like the blind, and we grope as if we had no eyes: we stumble at noonday as in the night; we are in desolate places as dead men* (Isaiah 59:4, 7-10).

Then, in this chapter foretelling our time, the final solution is given: *And the Redeemer shall come to Zion . . .* (verse 20). And, continuing: *Arise, shine; for thy light is come, and the glory of the* [Eternal] *is risen upon thee* (Isaiah 60:1).

The only hope of justice—of peace—of truth—of right solutions to all this world's problems, is the coming in power and glory of Christ to set up world government. Right government. The government of God!

In this, and many other passages, God shows in His Word to mankind how utterly helpless man is to govern himself and his fellows. Now 6,000 years of human experience has brought mankind to the very brink of world suicide. The world's leading scientists and statesmen say the only hope, now, is world government. I attended the San Francisco Conference in 1945, where world leaders attempted to form a world organization of nations. They called it "The United Nations." There I heard chiefs of state ring out the warning that this was the world's last chance.

46

But it has failed. The United Nations has no power over the nations. It has no power to settle disputes, stop wars, or prevent wars. The so-called United Nations are not united. This effort has degenerated into a sounding board for Communist propaganda. Man has failed his last chance!

Now God must step in—or we perish!

Sir Winston Churchill, before the United States Congress said, "There is a purpose being worked out here below." God Almighty had great purpose in creating the human family and placing us here on this earth. And He has a perfect master plan for accomplishing that Purpose.

That Master Plan involves a duration of 7,000 years. The seven literal days of Creation were a type. They set the pattern. The first six were days of physical creation. The seventh day of that first week began the spiritual creation, still going on. On that day God created His Sabbath, setting it apart as holy, for spiritual use. On that day God instructed the first man and woman in His spiritual truth. On that day He preached the Gospel to them, explaining about and offering them, freely, His wonderful gift of eternal life—symbolized by the "tree of life" in the Garden. He also explained that the wages of sin—rebellion against His government—was death.

With God, *one day is as a thousand years, and a thousand years is as one day* (II Peter 3:8).

So God allotted the first six thousand years to physical man, to live his own way (deceived and swayed by Satan), to prove by 6,000 years of suffering mountainous evils, that only God's way can bring desired blessings. That 6,000 years we may call "The Day of Man."

So, in other words, the first 6,000 years were allotted to allow Satan to labor at his work of deceiving the world, followed by 1,000 years (one millennial day) when Satan

47

shall not be allowed to do any of his "work" of deception. Put another way, God marked out six millennial days to allow man to indulge in the spiritual labor of sin, followed by a millennium of spiritual rest, under the enforced government of God.

Government Planned from Beginning

And now comes a wonderful truth.

Now we come to a revealed insight into the wonderful planning, preparing, and organizing of the perfect Government of God.

There will be no incompetent and selfishly ambitious politicians seeking to get their covetous hands on the throttle of government power by the deceptive political methods of this world. Today people are asked to vote into office men they know little about—men whose qualifications are largely misrepresented. In the soon-coming Government of God, every official placed in authority shall have been tried and tested, trained, experienced and qualified, by God's qualifications.

God has planned ahead, but not only for His government to rule the earth. He had said to Adam, in effect, "Go, plan your own human governments, create in your own imaginations your own gods and religions; develop your own knowledge and educational structure, plan your own social systems (in a word, organize your own human CIVILIZATION)."

But in sentencing man to 6,000 years of being cut off from God, He reserved the prerogative of calling to special service and contact with God such as He should choose for His purpose. During this Day of Man, God has prepared for His own millennial civilization, in all its phases—governmental, educational, religious—His whole civilization.

48

It all began with Abraham.

In his day, there was only one man on earth who was at once a man of strong character and at the same time meekly and wholly submissive and obedient to God—to God's Laws and His direction and rule. That man was Abraham.

God began training men for top positions of authority in His coming world, with Abraham. Abraham lived in the most advanced civilization—the most developed and, as people thought, most desirable locality.

God said to Abraham (then named Abram), *Get thee out of thy country, and from thy kindred, and from thy father's house, unto a land that I will shew thee* (Genesis 12:1).

There was no argument. Abraham didn't say, "But why? Why must I give up all the pleasures of this civilization—give up even my relatives and friends?" Abraham didn't argue or delay.

It is written, simply, *So Abram departed . . .* (verse 4).

Abraham was put to severe tests. But, after he died, God said, *. . . Abraham obeyed my voice, and kept my charge, my commandments, my statutes* [of government], *and my laws* (Genesis 26:5).

Abraham was being trained for high position in the Government of God, now soon to rule the world. He believed in, was obedient and loyal to, God's Government—its statutes and laws.

Abraham received the promises on which the salvation of every person, through Christ, is based. He is called the Father (humanly) of the faithful (Galatians 3:7). To the Gentiles of Galatia, the Apostle Paul wrote: *And if ye be Christ's, then are ye* [Gentiles] *Abraham's seed, and heirs according to the promise* (Galatians 3:29). In the 16th verse, he had said: *Now to Abraham and his seed* [descendant—Christ] *were the promises made. . . .*

49

God was starting to prepare for His Kingdom—to train topflight personnel for positions in God's civilization—with Abraham. When Abraham proved obedient, God blessed his labors and allowed him to become wealthy. God gave him experience in the wise handling of vast wealth, and in directing a great force of men under him.

Isaac was reared by God-fearing, God-obeying Abraham, in God's ways, obedient to God's Government. He became heir along with his father Abraham. He too, was trained in obedience, and also in directing and ruling over others.

Then Jacob, born with this rich heredity, was educated to follow through on the same pattern Abraham and Isaac had learned. Even though his father-in-law deceived him, and held him down, Jacob also became wealthy. He was human—as were Abraham and Isaac and all humans. He made mistakes. But he overcame. He repented. He prevailed with God. He never quit! He developed the qualities and character of leadership. He became the father of the twelve greatest nations-to-be in the soon-coming world tomorrow.

The Pattern of Government Organization

God has not told us, in so many words specifically, precisely how His coming world super government will be organized. Yet He has given us the general pattern. He has told us specifically where 14 high executives (including Christ) will fit in. And from them we may deduce a great deal of the remaining governmental structure. Much of the coming structure of government is at least strongly indicated by what is plainly revealed.

We know it will be the Government of God. God Almighty—the Father of Jesus Christ—is Supreme Lawgiver, and Head over Christ, and over all that is. We know that

Christ is to be King of kings, and Lord of lords—over both state and church, united through Him. We know that King David of ancient Israel (details later) will be King over the twelve great nations composed of literal descendants of the twelve tribes of Israel. We know the twelve apostles will each be a king, sitting on a throne, over one of those great nations descended from the tribes of Israel.

We know it will be government from the top down. There is to be a definite chain of authority. No one will be elected by the people. Mortal humans have proved they do not know how to judge qualifications, and do not know the inner minds, hearts, intents, and abilities, of men. All will be divinely appointed from above. All, in positions of governmental authority, will be resurrected immortals, born of God—no longer flesh-and-blood humans.

With this in mind—with the knowledge that Abraham is (humanly) the father of all who are Christ's and heirs of salvation—it becomes plain that Abraham will be given a greater position of authority in God's Kingdom than David—and that he will be over both Israelites and Gentiles. He is "father" of Gentile converts as well as Israelites.

Then again, repeatedly the Bible uses the phrase, "Abraham, Isaac and Jacob," grouping them together as a team, and calling them, together, "The Fathers." For the promises were repromised, also, to Isaac and Jacob, whose name was changed to Israel.

What is plainly revealed indicates, then, that Abraham, Isaac and Jacob, will function as a topflight team, with Abraham as chairman of the team, next under Christ in the coming world Government of God.

Jesus Himself said, definitely, that Abraham, Isaac and Jacob shall be in that glorious and glorified Kingdom (Luke 13:28).

Joseph qualified in a very special way, but we shall come back to him a little later.

Both Church and State

Another principle is made clear in God's Word: Church and State will be united under Christ. There will be one government, over all nations. There will be one church—one God—one religion—one educational system— one social order. And, as in God's original pattern in ancient Israel, they will be united.

Three men—Peter, James and John, among the original twelve disciples—were privileged to see the Kingdom of God in a vision (Matthew 17:9). In this vision, Jesus, who was actually with them in person, became transfigured— appearing as the glorified Christ. His face became bright, shining as the sun, His clothing white as light. Two others appeared with Him in this vision—this glimpse into the coming Kingdom—and they were Moses and Elijah. These two, in the vision, represented the offices of Church and State, with and under Christ, as they will be in God's Kingdom. Both Moses and Elijah qualified in their human lifetime for very high positions in the Kingdom of God. Moses was the one through whom Christ (yes, He was the God of the Old Testament, as many, many scriptures prove) gave the laws and the statutes of government for the nation Israel. Moses was trained as a son of Pharaoh, king of Egypt. His training and experience was among Gentiles, as well as the children of Israel.

Elijah, above all others, is represented in Scripture as the prophet who restored the worship of the true God—and obedience to His Commandments. When Elijah ordered King Ahab to gather on Mount Carmel *all Israel* (I Kings 18: 19-21) and the prophets of Baal and of Asherah (Easter), he said: *How long halt ye between two opinions? if the* [Eternal] *be God, follow him: but if Baal, then follow him.* And when, at Elijah's 18-second prayer (verses 36-37), the fire fell miraculously from heaven consuming Elijah's sacrifice, the people fell on their faces, and said, *The* [Eternal], *He is the God; The* [Eternal], *He is the God* (verse 39).

The vision of the Transfiguration (Matthew 16:27 through 17:9), gave the Apostles Peter, James, and John a preview of Christ coming in His Kingdom—as He shall come. The indication is thus given that Moses and Elijah represented the heads, under Christ, of state or national world government (under Moses), and church, or the worship or religious activity (under Elijah).

These two men, like the "fathers," Abraham, Isaac and Israel, will then be resurrected immortal, in power and glory. Certainly the indication is given us that, under Christ as King of kings, and under Christ's top team—the "fathers"— will be Moses over all organized national and international government; and Elijah, over all organized church, religious and educational activity.

Actually, the Gospel and religious development is merely spiritual education. And it is significant that Elijah had organized and headed three schools or colleges (II Kings 2:3, 5; 4:38—at Bethel, Jericho, and Gilgal) teaching God's Truth in a world corrupted by false pagan education.

On the National Level

Now we gain further insight into God's coming world government organization.

On the purely national level, the nations descended from the two tribes of Ephraim and Manasseh (descended from Joseph), will become the two leading nations of the

53

world (Jeremiah 30:16-18; 31:4-11, 18-20; Isaiah 14:1-8; Deuteronomy 28:13).

But, next to them will be the nations descended from the other tribes of Israel. And, after them, but still prosperous and full of abundant blessings, the Gentile nations.

King David, resurrected, immortal, in power and glory, will be king, under Moses, over all twelve nations of Israel (Jeremiah 30:9; Ezekiel 34:23-24; 37:24-25). Each of the original twelve apostles will be king, under David, over one of these then super-prosperous nations (Matthew 19:28).

Under the apostles, each now king over a great nation, will be the rulers over districts, states, shires, counties or provinces, and over cities.

But, in every case, these kings and rulers will be resurrected immortals, born into the Kingdom (Family) of God as Spirit beings—not flesh-and-blood mortals. And, in every case, they will be those who qualified not only by conversion, but by overcoming, spiritual character development, growth in Christ's knowledge—training in being ruled by God's Laws and government, as well as learning to rule.

The parables of the pounds (Luke 19:11-27) and talents (Matthew 25:14-30) make this very clear. The one who multiplied his spiritual abilities ten times over is pictured as ruling over ten cities. The one who developed only half as much in God's character and abilities is pictured as being given rule over five cities. The parable of the talents shows the same thing, but also we are to be judged by how well we do with what we have to do *with*. That is, one of lesser ability will be judged according to motivation, application, diligence, and persistence according to ability. To whom much—in natural ability, and spiritual gifts—is inherited and given, much will be required. The one of lesser ability stands just as good a

54

chance for reward in God's Kingdom as the one of great ability—if he tries as hard.

But what of all the Gentile nations? Who will be given top positions of rule over them?

There is strong indication—not a definite, specific statement—but indication, according to principles and specific assignments that are revealed, that the Prophet Daniel will be made king over them all, directly under Moses. What prophet—what man of God—did God send to be trained at top-level government authority, in the world's very first world empire? And what man refused to follow pagan ways and customs, even while serving next in authority to the king himself? What man proved loyal to God, and the worship of God, and obedient to the laws of God—even while serving at the top in the first world empire?

Why, of course it was the prophet Daniel.

At first thought, one might suppose Christ will put the Apostle Paul at the head—under Moses and under Christ—of all Gentile nations. And indeed Paul qualified for high position over Gentiles.

But Daniel was thrown into almost daily contact with the king in the world's first world government. And though that was human government, Daniel proved completely loyal and obedient to God and God's rule. He was used, to reveal to King Nebuchadnezzar, and immediate successors, that it is God who rules over all kingdoms. Daniel refused the king's rich food and delicacies—including what was unclean according to God's health laws. He prayed three times a day to God, even though it meant being thrown into the den of lions. He trusted God to protect and deliver him from the lions. He gained knowledge and wisdom in the affairs and administration of government over nations.

When God, through the prophet Ezekiel, named three

of the most righteous men who ever lived, He named Daniel as one of them. The other two were Noah and Job (Ezekiel 14:14, 20). And it is evident that God will assign Noah and Job to offices of very great magnitude. More of that, later.

God in His Word gave Daniel the assurance that he shall be in the Kingdom of God, at the time of resurrection (Daniel 12:13).

It is an interesting possibility, in passing, to consider that Daniel's three colleagues in this Chaldean Empire service—Shadrach, Meshach, and Abednego—might serve as a team directly with and under Daniel, even as the three "Fathers" very possibly may serve as a team directly with and under Christ Himself. In fact there are a number of such teams which appear to be possibilities.

But what about Paul? As the twelve original apostles were sent to the "lost" House of Israel, Paul was the apostle to the Gentiles. That is the key. Christ Himself said specifically that each of the twelve shall be a king over one of the nations of Israel. It is inconceivable that Paul would be over no more than one Gentile nation. It might even be inferred that Paul rated a little higher in ability and accomplishment than any one of the Twelve Apostles. And, again, no Gentile nation will be as great as one of the Israelite nations.

The indication, then, seems to be that Paul will be given position over all Gentile nations, but under Daniel.

Of course there will be kings appointed by Christ over every Gentile nation. And district rulers under them, and rulers over cities. There is no indication as to the identity of any of these, except that those apostles and evangelists who worked with and directly under Paul—Barnabas, Silas, Timothy, Titus, Luke, Mark, Philemon, etc. undoubtedly will be given offices of importance. And what of other saints of that same time, in the first flush years of the Church, when its membership at first multiplied in number of converts? And what of many converted since, and down to our present day?

We can mention, here, only what seems to be rather clearly indicated from what God has already revealed.

The International Level

Beside these revealed and indicated assignments of government over nations and groups of nations on the national level, there will be positions of great magnitude on the international level in the areas of scientific and social functions. And there are a few indications of what some of those operations will be, and the possible—if not probable— personnel.

Since Noah lived first, we now take a look at Noah. In Noah's day, the chief cause of the violence and chaos of world conditions was racial hatreds, interracial marriages, and racial violence caused by man's efforts toward integration and amalgamation of races, contrary to God's laws. God had set the boundary lines for the nations and the races at the beginning (Deuteronomy 32:8-9; Acts 17:26). But men had refused to remain in the lands to which God had assigned them. That was the cause of the corruption and violence that ended that world. For 120 years Noah had preached God's ways to the people—but they didn't heed.

At that time, even as today, that world faced a population explosion. It was when *men began to multiply on the face of the earth* (Genesis 6:1). Jesus said, of our time, right now, *But as the days of Noe* [Noah] *were, so shall the coming of the Son of man be* (Matthew 24:37)—or, as in Luke 17:26, *And as it was in the days of Noe, so shall it be also in the days of the Son of man.* That is, the days just before Christ returns. Today race wars, race hatreds, race riots, and race problems are among the world's greatest social troubles.

Noah merely preached to people in his human lifetime. But Noah, in the resurrection, immortal, in power and glory, will be given the power to enforce God's ways in regard to race.

It seems evident that the resurrected Noah will head a vast project of the relocation of the races and nations, within the boundaries God has set, for their own best good, happiness, and richest blessings. This will be a tremendous operation. It will require great and vast organization, reinforced with power to move whole nations and races. This time, peoples and nations will move where God has planned for them, and no defiance will be tolerated.

What a paradox. People are going to be forced to be happy, to have peace, to find abundant and joyful living!

Above, we said we would come back, later, to Joseph, son of Israel and great-grandson of Abraham.

Joseph became food administrator of the greatest nation on earth of that time—Egypt. Joseph was synonymous with "prosperity." *And the* [Eternal] *was with Joseph, and he was a prosperous man; and . . . the* [Eternal] *made all that he did to prosper in his hand* (Genesis 39:2-3). He was made actual ruler for the Pharaoh of the world's greatest nation. But his specialty was dealing with the economy—with prosperity. And what he did, he did God's way.

It seems evident, therefore, that Joseph will be made director of the world's economy—its agriculture, its industry, its technology, and its commerce—as well as its money and monetary system. These systems will be on the international level, the same in every nation.

Undoubtedly Joseph will develop a large and perfectly efficient organization of immortals made perfect, with and under him in this vast administration. This will be an administration that will eliminate famine, starvation, poverty. There will be no poverty-stricken slums. There will be universal prosperity!

Another tremendous project on the worldwide international level will be that of rebuilding the waste places, and the construction of whatever really great and large buildings or structures Christ will require for the world He will create. *And they shall build the old wastes, they shall raise up the former desolations, and they shall repair the waste cities, the desolations of many generations* (Isaiah 61:4).

Job was the wealthiest and greatest man of the east (Job 1:3) and a noted builder. (Compare Job 3:14 with God's challenge in Job 38:4-6.) He was so upright and perfect, God even dared Satan to find a flaw in his character. Actually, there was a terrible sin in his life—self-righteousness. But God brought him to repentance. (See Job chapters 38-42.) Once this man, of such strength of self-mastery that he could be so righteous in his own strength, was humbled, brought to reliance on God, filled with God's Spirit—well, surely no man who ever lived could equal him as an engineer over vast stupendous world projects.

Indication is strong, therefore, that Job will be director of worldwide urban renewal, rebuilding the waste places and the destroyed cities, not as they are now, but according to God's pattern; vast engineering projects, such as dams and power plants—or whatever the ruling Christ shall decree.

At least one man seems indicated as a top assistant in this vast administration. That is Zerubbabel (Haggai, and Zechariah 4).

So much for the new world super-civilization on the national and international level.

Now we come to the world tomorrow on the individual level—the church—the religion—the educational system.

5

Education and Religion Tomorrow

WHEN JESUS CHRIST RETURNS
to earth in the full supreme power
and glory of the Creator God, He is
coming, this time, to save the world, spiritually.

When He sits on the throne of His glory, in Jerusalem,
all nations composed of flesh-and-blood mortal humans will
be there before Him. He shall begin dividing "His sheep
from the goats." To the sheep, on His right hand, *Then shall
the King say unto them on his right hand, Come, ye blessed of
my Father, inherit the kingdom prepared for you from the
foundation of the world* (Matthew 25:31-34).

Those converted, now, are heirs. We shall inherit the
Kingdom at Christ's coming. The dead in Christ shall be
resurrected, rising first—changed to Spirit immortality. We
which are then alive, in Christ, shall be instantaneously

changed to Spirit immortality, and caught up with the resurrected ones, to meet the descending Christ in the air.

We shall then be separated by immortality from the mortal humans on earth.

Wherever Jesus is, from there, we shall be ever with Him. Where, then, will He be? His feet shall stand that same day on the Mount of Olives (Zechariah 14:4).

It is after this that He separates the sheep—(those who repent, believe, and receive His Holy Spirit)—from the goats—(those who rebel). This separation—this winning converts for God's Kingdom—will continue throughout the entire thousand years of Christ's reign on earth.

Christ will give to all nations a new and pure language, *that they may all call upon the name of the* [Eternal], *to serve him with one consent* (Zephaniah 3:9).

The pure truth of God will be proclaimed to all people. No one will be deceived any longer. But *the earth shall be full of the knowledge of the* [Eternal], *as the waters cover the sea* (Isaiah 11:9).

Christ is the *root of Jesse*, father of David. To Christ, then, will the Gentiles seek (Isaiah 11:10). Christ will set His hand to save all Israel (verse 11). (Also Romans 11:25-26.)

But all this work of world evangelism—of spiritually saving the world (as a whole, not necessarily every individual—but surely a majority)—will require, first, and with it, reeducating the world.

Close to half of all people on earth today are illiterate. They are so ignorant they simply could not be given even what might be called bare "saving knowledge." A man in a country in the interior of Central Africa had heard *The World Tomorrow* program on Radio Elisabethville. He was a steady listener, and he received *The* Plain Truth magazine. He wrote us letters. He wanted to represent this Work of

God, and raise up a church among his people. We sent two ministers stationed in London to visit this man, get to know him, and determine by personal contact what should be done. They found he was the only man of any education among them. The others were illiterate people. They were so ignorant, it was impossible for them to comprehend anything about God, or Christ, or salvation. Sadly, our ministers said such people would have to receive at least elementary education before they could be reached with the Gospel.

Reeducating the World

But now consider those in our more universally educated affluent nations—the United States, Britain, Canada, Australia, Germany, France, and such nations.

We covered a section on this world's paganized, agnostic, decadent education earlier in this book. The academic system was founded by the pagan philosopher Plato. It has always remained pagan. Injected into it, in more recent times, has been German rationalism, and the atheistic theory of evolution.

Evolution, the atheist's explanation of a creation without a Creator, is the basic concept on which modern education has been built. Modern education is a mixture of truth and error, fact and fable.

The educated of this world started, at birth, from scratch, so far as knowledge goes. At the hour of birth, they knew nothing. The process of education in this world is one of funneling knowledge into minds. It is a process of memorizing. The student is taught from texts. Textbooks are supposed to be true and authoritative. The student must read, study, accept and memorize. In exams he is graded on the accuracy of repeating what was "in the book." He is not supposed to question, but to accept and believe.

Modern education has been based on a false, erroneous, untrue foundation. The supposedly educated of this world—even the great minds—have absorbed false knowledge. They have been trained in a false approach to knowledge. Almost always, error is based on a false assumed premise or hypothesis, taken for granted, never questioned—and, of course, unproved. The "educated" minds have been filled with such false hypotheses. They have allowed a false sense of values to flood their minds.

Truth appears to them to be fable. What is right may be to them foolishness. That which may be utterly wrong appears to be right. They come to view things through the false concept of evolution.

This mis-education holds their minds captive.

It has been explained how the natural *carnal* mind, devoid of revealed knowledge from God, is limited to knowledge of the physical and material. The approach to all knowledge in the Western world has been through the evolutionary hypothesis—never through God's revealed knowledge.

In God's millennial civilization, the basis of all knowledge dissemination will be revelation. Light will replace darkness—truth will replace error. Understanding will replace crass materialism. True knowledge will replace intellectual ignorance.

Many years ago, I handed a comparatively brief paper, disproving the evolutionary theory, to a scientist, asking for comment. This was the approximate comment: "Mr. Armstrong, you appear to have an uncanny knack of getting immediately to the trunk of the tree, and its roots, avoiding all the little twiggy propositions dependent on the trunk. You chop down the trunk, pull out the roots, and all supporting equations come crashing down. I have to admit you have chopped down the entire tree. Yet I have to go on believing evolution. All my life has been devoted to science and philosophy based on evolution. I have done graduate work and post-doctorate work at some of our highest-rated universities. I have been continually in contact with scientists, and have absorbed that atmosphere completely. I am so steeped in it I would be utterly unable to disbelieve in the evolutionary process, even though you disprove it."

One of the great problems facing the returned glorified Christ, will be that of reeducating the supposedly educated. These minds—and they are, indeed, the world's finest and best minds, have become so perverted with false education that they will be unable to accept truth until they first *un*-learn error. And it is at least ten times more difficult to unlearn error, firmly imbedded in the mind, than it is to start from "scratch" and learn new truth.

It may actually take them longer to come to a knowledge of truth—to become truly educated—than the illiterate of this world.

God's inspired Word, the Holy Bible, is the foundation of knowledge. But they have been trained to hold this true foundation in prejudiced contempt.

Yes, indeed, the educating and reeducating of the world will be one of the most important tasks the Kingdom of God will face, after Christ returns to rule. Today people follow the false and deceptive values. Their entire thinking will require a reorientation—a change of direction.

A Headquarters Church

We have seen that the earth, after this thousand-year-period begins, will be as full of the true knowledge of God as the oceans are full of water (Isaiah 11:9). How will this be brought about?

The Prophet Micah gives part of the answer: *But in the*

last days it shall come to pass, that the mountain of the house of the [Eternal] *shall be established in the top of the mountains, and shall be exalted above the hills; and people shall flow unto it* (Micah 4:1).

Prophecy uses "mountain" as a symbol of a major nation, and "hills" as a symbol of smaller nations. In other words, the Kingdom of God, the Kingdom of resurrected immortals—the ruling Kingdom—will be established in complete authority over the major nations (of mortals) and exalted above the small nations—and people will flow to God's Kingdom. Now continue:

And many nations shall come, and say, Come, and let us go up to the mountain of the [Eternal], *and to the house of the God of Jacob; and he will teach us of his ways, and we will walk in his paths: for the law shall go forth of Zion* [the Church] *and the Word of the* [Eternal] *from Jerusalem. And he* [Christ] *shall judge among many people, and rebuke strong nations afar off; and they shall beat their swords into plowshares, and their spears into pruninghooks: nation shall not lift up a sword against nation, neither shall they learn war any more* (verses 2-3).

This knowledge—this teaching—and even knowledge of God's Law—shall go forth from the Church—and from Jerusalem, the new world capital.

We add another fact revealed in Acts 15. A misunderstanding had arisen about certain doctrinal duties in the Church at Antioch. This was in the early days of the New Testament Church of God. The pattern is there revealed that there was a Headquarters Church at Jerusalem. The Apostles Peter and James, and other top-ranking ministers were there. So the matter was taken to this Headquarters Church for authoritative instruction.

Gathered there for this conference were the Headquar-

65

ters apostles, plus Paul, and the elders. Even so, there was sharp contention and much disputing. Then Peter, chief apostle, rose and gave God's inspired decision. The Church received its teachings from the apostles. But in the Kingdom, Jesus Christ Himself will be there to lead His Headquarters Church. At Jerusalem, James was pastor. And as a matter of protocol to make Peter's decision official, James approved it and wrote up the official authoritative document.

This chapter discloses the pattern.

Christ, Himself, will be ruling from Jerusalem. Stationed there with Christ, under immediate direction of Elijah, it is indicated, will be those immortals chosen by Christ to constitute the Headquarters Church. Revelation 3:12 indicates those of this "Philadelphia" era will be pillars in that Headquarters Church.

Next, in this all-important Headquarters Church organization, working with and directly under Elijah, it appears, will be the resurrected John the Baptist. He came *in the power and spirit of Elias* [Elijah] (Luke 1:17). Of him, Jesus said, *Verily I say unto you, Among them that are born of women there hath not risen a greater than John the Baptist . . .* (Matthew 11:11). He was the *Elijah* prophesied to come (Matthew 17:10-13; and 11:7-11).

Jesus said that no man who ever lived was greater than John the Baptist. Yet, even the least in the resurrected Kingdom will be greater (Matt. 11:11). It is evident that John the Baptist will be placed in very high office. It seems logical that he should be placed with, or immediately under, Elijah.

This Headquarters Church, at Christ's own world capital of Jerusalem, then, undoubtedly will be given the administration of the world's new system of education.

Also the indication is that the teaching of spiritual truth—of the true gospel, the spiritual conversion of the world—will be directed, worldwide, from this Headquarters Church, under Elijah and the overall direct supervision of Jesus Christ.

The principal purpose for which Christ is returning to earth is to spiritually develop in humanity Godly character, and to save the world. Most religious people, ministers, and evangelists (fundamentalist), have supposed that this time, now, is the only day of salvation. The verse of Scripture they rely on is a mistranslation (II Corinthians 6:2). It should read *"a* day of salvation," not *"the"* (quoted from Isaiah 49:8, where it is *a* not *the*). If Christ had been trying to "save" the world, He would have saved the world. It hasn't been "saved." God doesn't use a babylon of confused, disagreeing religious organizations, divided into hundreds of different concepts of theological doctrine, as His instruments.

But the real world evangelism will be administered by this Headquarters Church, composed of resurrected immortals, under direct personal supervision of Christ Himself.

One thing there will not be in the millennial Headquarters Church is a doctrinal committee of intellectual "scholars" to decide whether Christ's teachings are true doctrines.

There was no such doctrinal committee in the first century Headquarters Church at Jerusalem. All teaching came from Christ through the apostles—and a few times Christ communicated to apostles via the prophets (of which there are none in God's Church today)—since the Bible for our time is complete. God's Church today, as in the first century, receives its teachings from the living Christ, through an apostle, just as in A.D. 31.

One other tremendous organizational function will be directed from this Headquarters Church—that of direction of all the churches over the world. These churches will be composed of those who become converted—begotten of God by receiving His Holy Spirit—though still mortal.

Just as the converted Christian in this present age must continue to live a life of overcoming, and of spiritual growth and development (II Peter 3:18), so will they in the Millennium. Happily they then will not have to overcome Satan. But they shall have to overcome all evil impulses, habits, or temptations, innate within themselves.

With only one Church—one religion—one faith—there will be many church congregations in every city, others scattered through rural areas. There will be district superintendents over areas, and pastors, elders, deacons and deaconesses in every local church.

This, then, gives an insight into how the world will be organized.

This shows how a super world government can, and will, be established on earth.

Why Supernatural Force

World leaders today are virtually unanimous in concluding that man's only hope of being saved alive for even another generation lies in establishing an all-powerful super world government. Yet all confess that nations are utterly unable to bring it about.

Sir Winston Churchill once said: "The creation of an authoritative all-powerful world order is the ultimate aim toward which we must strive. Unless some effective world super government can be brought quickly into action, the proposals for peace and human progress are dark and doubtful."

Clement Attlee, a former British Prime Minister, said: "The world needs the consummation of our conception of world organization through world law if civilization is to survive!" Again he said, "We have not an awful lot of time. There is too much dangerous stuff in the world, and there are too many fools about, trigger-happy idiots and the like."

We could reproduce such quotes from world leaders, past and present, for the next hundred pages. But all know that man is utterly helpless and unable to bring about such a solution.

Would the United States say to the leaders of other nations, "We are ready to relinquish all sovereignty over ourselves, and place our great nation under the absolute rule of leaders from Russia, China, France, Egypt, and other countries"? Would the leaders in the Kremlin step down, and relinquish all Communist sovereignty to a government headed by leaders from the United States, and these other countries?

And, if men should undertake to establish a super world government, wielding all the military power over all nations, what form of government would the nations submit to? The men in the Kremlin would never step down in submission unless this world government would be Russian communism—and even then, these men in the Kremlin would insist on having all the power. But the Chinese communists would not submit to that—they would demand that the new world government be their brand of Communism.

Most nations would never accept democracy as the form of world government, and the United States would accept nothing else.

Could anything be more impossible than for this world's nations to get together, in a new world government of some form, each surrendering all its power and sovereignty to it?

No, and even when Almighty God, the Creator and

Ruler over the entire universe, does supernaturally intervene to set up His world government—His perfect Government—the nations will be angry. The nations will fight. Men will say, "We don't want God to rule over us!"

That's why Christ is coming in all the power and glory of God's supernatural force. That's why He will rule *with a rod of iron*. Man will never submit to the way of peace, prosperity, happiness, and abundant well-being unless he is forced into it!

Purposed Long Ago

But God Almighty is working out a purpose here below.

And the Eternal God carefully planned every move toward the accomplishment of that purpose.

His first promise of this happy state was made to Abraham. God promised Abraham this whole earth as an everlasting inheritance for him and his children. God promised that through Abraham all nations of the earth would be blessed.

At the same time, God began insuring the efficiency and perfection of His world-ruling government by causing Abraham, Isaac, Israel and Joseph to be trained—during a lifetime—in several basic essentials for top personnel in a government of perfection.

First is right attitude. That is essential. God looks on the heart—the spirit—the attitude. That is where He looked in choosing David to be King over Israel (I Samuel 16:6-7). That is where He looks in you, and in me. These men were trained in submission to God and those over them in authority. They were trained in teamwork—in harmoniously working together.

Secondly, they were trained in knowledge of the true values.

After that, they were trained in handling people, in wise management of people, of wealth—without letting it turn their heads.

In the same way, King David was trained and developed.

All who, made immortal, will occupy important executive offices in the coming world super government were trained in these essentials. All realize fully not only the power, but the wisdom, the love, the holiness and perfection of Almighty God. All know of a certainty that His ways are the right ways—His Laws, the right and perfect Laws—His Rule and His Government, the perfect government that will bring every blessing to those whom they govern.

In this way, the Everliving God has prepared for His Kingdom. He began, long ago, selecting men of outstanding ability who would yield fully to Him, inculcating into their innermost being those principles and characteristics that form the seven basic laws for success in life.

1) The right goal—to be born into God's Kingdom—the goal which inspires motivation and stimulates the ambition to achieve that goal.

2) The right teaching or education. Every one of these men was freed from the shackles of pagan teaching, tradition, erroneous knowledge, sense of false values, and pagan customs. Every one was trained in God's ways, based on God's Laws, and the principles of those Laws. They were trained in the ways of righteousness. They became skilled in applying the principles of God's Commandments, laws, statutes and judgments.

3) They were trained in the development of good health—avoiding the causes of sickness, disease, infirmities. They were trained in keeping their minds sharp, clear, alert, balanced, sound.

4) Every one was trained in developing drive—con-

71

stantly putting a prod on self, not only to accomplish more, strive harder, but to drive the self away from wrong desires, impulses, or temptations, and into the right ways of God's Law. They were trained to flee temptation. They were all human. They all did sin—sometimes seriously—but they repented; they profited by mistakes; they overcame these things.

5) These men were schooled through a lifetime in resourcefulness. God allowed multiple problems, hazards, obstacles to confront them—to try the mettle of these men. They learned how to face up to and solve problems—not to be defeated by them.

6) These men endured. They kept their eyes constantly on the goal. When the going got so tough that even with their resourcefulness they could not think their way through—when it appeared they were completely defeated, when it appeared hopeless to try to carry on further, they did not give up—they never quit! They endured through thick and thin—they endured to the end. They endured by faith in God.

7) And, along with these traits, these men relied on the guidance and the help of God. They walked with God. They talked to God. They listened to God—whether He spoke verbally and in person, or through His Scriptures. They sought wisdom from God. They relied on God for guidance, for protection, for every need. They submitted to, and obeyed God.

Compare with Today's Politicians

And now—finally. Consider!

Take outstanding, superior men, having undergone a human lifetime of this attitude, this training in the ways of success and perfection. But now change these men by a resurrection into the perfection of immortality.

72

And consider that immortality will multiply their aptitudes, abilities and powers perhaps a million times above what they achieved as humans, by infusing into them the power and glory of God.

That is what God is going to do!

And there you have the chief executive personnel, under Christ, administering the new super world government.

Compare that to the scheming, compromising, selfishly motivated politicians that head most of the governments of this world today and other phases of civilization.

Feast your eyes for a while on the picture of the world tomorrow which God's Government will produce—as we shall now do—and when you take your eyes from this book, and look again on this drab, ugly, sin-sick world of corruption, violence and suffering—it will make you sick at heart.

But doesn't it make you want to shout for joy, to realize what a civilization—what a world—is actually coming?

Doesn't it make you want to really put your heart into your prayers, praying earnestly, *"Oh God! Thy kingdom come! Thy will be done on earth, as it is in heaven!"*

Just a few general afterthoughts before we leave the subject of the personnel and organization of the coming Kingdom.

One may well ask: "What of such men as Abel, and Enoch?" You read of them, in the faith chapter—Hebrews 11—as men of faith and righteousness (verses 4, 5). We answer: God has not revealed to us where they will be placed. We have mentioned here only those few where there appears to be real scriptural indication, based on what is revealed, as to what posts they will fill in the Kingdom. This same 11th chapter of Hebrews implies, certainly, that others such as the harlot Rahab, Gideon, Barak, Samson, Jephthae, and Samuel will be in God's Kingdom. We cannot

73

presume to decide what office Christ has in store for them. And there are many, many others.

It is one of the joys of anticipation to realize that we shall know where they shall be placed in the near future.

Someone may ask, "What about the women?" Yes, there were outstanding women—Sarah, Rebecca, Rachel. There were Miriam, Deborah, and others. In the Kingdom, there will be no sex—no male and female (Matthew 22:30). Women, then, will be the same as men.

Sarah is called the mother of righteous women in the New Testament (I Peter 3:6). Deborah actually judged, or ruled Israel for a time. Their status in the Kingdom will be the same as men. We would certainly suppose that women such as these will be given high position and great honor in the Kingdom. But we do not presume, in this present writing, to suggest what it shall be.

6

Now Picture Tomorrow's World!

WE HAVE COVERED SOMETHING OF the organization of the government that will rule tomorrow's world.

Now picture the changed conditions!

Look now at the solved problems!

See, now, a glimpse into a world of no illiteracy, no poverty, no famine and starvation, into a world where crime decreases rapidly, people learn honesty, chastity, human kindness, and happiness—a world of peace, prosperity, abundant well-being.

The Population Explosion Solved

God predicts vast reforms everywhere in the wonderful utopian era He says will soon break out on this earth.

Can you imagine it? A world of great strides in solving the most crucial problems facing mankind.

Today—the greatest and most awesome problem of all is the population explosion. Growing populations in all nations are rapidly outstripping the ability of the world to sustain them.

And the areas of the greatest rise in population are the underdeveloped parts of the world—the "have-not" nations of poverty, illiteracy, disease and superstition. Remember, not more than 10 percent of the earth's surface is tillable, or arable, land. And now the latest UN figures indicate the world will double in population in just 35 short years.

The daily, ominous pressure of people is one of the truly incomprehensible problems today.

But God has the solution, and how simple it is. Simply make most of the earth cultivatable. Reduce the bare, snow-swept and craggy mountains, raise up some of the deep, arid desert valleys, change the world weather patterns. Make all the deserts green and fertile. Open up huge slices of the earth, like the Kalahari Desert, the Lake Chad basin and the Sahara, in Africa, the Gobi Desert in Asia, and the great American deserts. Make green and verdant the vast wastes of Mongolia, Siberia, Saudi Arabia and many of the Western states in the U.S.

Thaw out the deep ice packs and snowdrifts, the permafrost and tundra from the vast, almost limitless expanses of Antarctica, North America, Greenland, Northern Europe and Siberia. Make level the awesome Pamir Knot, the huge giants of the Himalayas, the Atlas, Taurus, Pyrenees, Rockies, Sierras and Hindu Kush—level the immense sweep of the Andes, and all the other forbidding, towering, virtually uninhabitable mountains of earth.

Then, provide good, gentle rainfall, in right balance, just at the right season.

And what happens?

Multiple millions of acres of unbelievably fertile, productive, wonderful farmland suddenly become available—just waiting to be discovered, and pioneered.

Impossible?

In the hands of man—certainly.

But look what God promises. *Fear not, thou worm Jacob, and ye men of Israel; I will help thee, saith the* [Eternal], *and thy redeemer, the Holy One of Israel.*

Behold, I will make thee a new sharp threshing instrument having teeth: thou shalt thresh the mountains, and beat them small, and shalt make the hills as chaff. Thou shalt fan them, and the wind shall carry them away, and the whirlwind shall scatter them: and thou shalt rejoice in the [Eternal], *and shalt glory in the Holy One of Israel.*

When the poor and needy seek water, and there is none, and their tongue faileth for thirst, I the [Eternal] *will hear them, I the God of Israel will not forsake them. I will open rivers in high places, and fountains* [artesian wells] *in the midst of the valleys: I will make the wilderness a pool of water, and the dry land springs of water.*

I will plant in the wilderness the cedar, the shittah [acacia] *tree, and the myrtle and the oil tree; I will set in the desert the fir tree, and the pine, and the box tree* [cypress] *together: That they may see, and know, and consider, and understand together, that the hand of the* [Eternal] *hath done this, and the Holy One of Israel hath created it.* (Isaiah 41:14-20).

Pure Water—Fertile Deserts.

Can you imagine such a fabulous scene? Deserts becoming green, fertile, garden lands of trees, shrubs, bubbling springs and brooks; mountains brought low, and made inhabitable.

Notice how God describes these conditions in many parts of the Bible.

Then shall the lame man leap as an hart, and the tongue of the dumb sing: for in the wilderness shall waters break out, and streams in the desert. And the parched ground shall become a pool, and the thirsty land springs of water: in the habitation of dragons [jackals], *where each lay, shall be grass with reeds and rushes* (Isaiah 35:6-7).

Read the whole 35th chapter of Isaiah.

God says, *The wilderness and the solitary place shall be glad for them; and the desert shall rejoice, and blossom as the rose. It shall blossom abundantly, and rejoice even with joy and singing . . .* (verses 1-2).

Some years ago, in a dry, dusty canyon deep in the profusion of hills between Bakersfield and Los Angeles, California, a minor earthquake struck. The proprietors of a small resort, now almost totally ignored, and nearly always deserted because of the parched conditions of the area, were considering closing up and moving elsewhere.

Suddenly, a groaning, jolting earthquake rippled through the arid hills. Not long after the earth rocked and groaned beneath their feet, they heard a faint gurgling sound. They ran to the dry, dusty creek bed that coursed through their property—and were utterly amazed to see *water* flowing swiftly along. As the creek gradually cleared up, they found the water to be crystal clear and pure—sweet and refreshing to drink.

Needless to say, their business picked up again.

Somehow, the earthquake had broken open an underground water source, sending it cascading through their property.

Think about the vast wastes of this earth. Does it sound incredible, unbelievable that God could make them blossom like a rose? Why should it?

The mountains were formed. Great forces caused gigantic upheavals, or huge cracks and slippages in the crust of the earth. Massive blocks of granite lunged up into the sky—the earth rocking and reeling in the throes of the greatest earthquakes in its history. Mountains were made—they didn't just happen.

The God of all power, who formed the hills and mountains (Amos 4:13; Psalm 90:2), will re-form them—will re-shape the surface of this earth.

Read of the huge earthquakes yet to come which will directly accomplish much of the rehabilitation of the land surfaces. (See Revelation 16:18; Zechariah 14:4.) God says, *The mountains quake at him, and the hills melt . . .* (Nahum 1:5).

Land Beneath Sea Reclaimed

Man recognizes much of the wealth of the world lies beneath the seas. Oil, gold, silver, and dozens of minerals—these all remain unobtainable today, lying untapped deep under the vast oceans. Also, seawater contains a great deal of gold and most of the world's gold supplies are under the oceans.

Many areas of the earth are ravaged by tidal action—by the ceaseless pounding of the surf that gradually wears away additional land. The lowlands of Europe, Holland in particular, consist to quite an extent of land reclaimed from the sea.

Think of the multiple millions of additional acres available to mankind if some of the world's oceans were reduced in size. And God says they shall be! Notice it, *And the* [Eternal] *shall utterly destroy the tongue of the Egyptian sea; and with his mighty wind shall he shake his hand over the river, and shall smite it in the seven streams, and make men go over dryshod* (Isaiah 11:15).

79

Sounds incredible—but it's true!

Today, the United States realizes water shortages are becoming critical. Wasted water through the huge consumption of industry—through pollution—and through the prodigious amounts used by each person each day, mean the ominous approach of that day when water is scarce.

As a result, additional huge dams are planned—fantastically expensive seawater conversion plants being constructed. So far, however, the cost of desalinization is completely prohibitive. But God describes a wonderful era of discovery and invention in the world tomorrow—major portions of the earth reclaimed and put to productive use.

The problems of the population explosion are real and manifold. Not only does mass starvation face millions within the foreseeable future, but government leaders recognize there is an even more immediate concern. Food wars.

Witness what happened in India. Government troops once battled 100,000 people who were rioting because of the slaughter of "sacred" cows in their country—done, in part, in an attempt to stave off starvation for those same rioters.

You see, there are more cattle in India than in the U.S. Yet, because of religious beliefs, the cattle are not eaten. They wander about the fields, and into the villages and towns, eating prodigious amounts of food, some of which would be edible for humans. The cattle are not used for any constructive purpose.

In addition to this, some years ago terrible floods and long-term drought in many areas produced grain shortages more severe than usual. Fully half of India's crops traditionally have been lost as well through lack of adequate transportation and storage facilities, to rodent and insect damage and by being siphoned off to the black market. As a result, India asked the United States for help.

The largest peacetime armada in all man's history was assembled—over six hundred ships—and began plying the oceans between U.S. ports and India. Quickly, the vast wheat reserves of the United States were depleted. But the famine in India was only barely staved off for one season. And any sudden disasters in American wheat areas could mean threatening famine in the United States—because we have insufficient reserves.

But what about the following years?

Government leaders fear huge food wars may be fought—each nation struggling mightily to possess the dwindling means of survival—food and water.

Sickness and Disease Feared

A horrifying "solution" to the population explosion may right now be in the making, unless God averts it.

With growing malnutrition and starvation comes the macabre threat of disease epidemics of massive, worldwide proportions. Already, officials warn of the threat of vast epidemics of cholera, typhoid, tuberculosis, flu, or even the dread "black death" (bubonic plague) that took the lives of millions in Europe during the 15th through the 17th centuries, and in the huge plague that ravaged England in 1664 and 1665.

But God says disease and sickness will finally be conquered.

That is the express aim of all the vast medical and pharmaceutical companies today—the final conquering of the ills, sicknesses and diseases of mankind.

Medical science seeks to find cures for sickness—cures for flu, and the common cold—cures for cancer, sclerosis, heart disease, arthritis, deafness and blindness, muscular dystrophy, epilepsy, and all the other pain-ridden debilities of man.

Let's understand the real meaning of this word "cure." Do you realize that cures for diseases already contracted merely mean rendering God's Laws ineffectual? It means ignoring the cause—allowing people to perpetrate the cause—and then treating only the effect. It means continuing to break nature's laws which God has made to operate in the human body, and then trying to prevent nature's laws from exacting their penalties.

But God shows that, when His Kingdom rules, He will teach people to obey nature's laws—stop causing sickness and disease. In other words, stop sinning—because sin is defined as transgressing God's laws (I John 3:4).

God reveals a great result of the increased productivity of the land, and the abundance of right and good foods, together with right knowledge and education in health laws, will be good health for all.

The dream of conscientious doctors may be to put themselves out of a job, by finding cures for every sickness and disease. But let's face it! To ignore the cause and merely treat the effect—to tacitly encourage people to continue causing sickness and disease by neglecting to educate them against it—could only perpetuate the medical profession. Can we have utopia with people causing themselves sickness and disease, secure in the delusion that medical "science" can remove the penalty?

In God's new world tomorrow, there will, indeed, probably be a place for doctors. But it will be teaching people to keep well, by avoiding the causes of disease. That will require an entirely new type of medical education—only we shall then drop the term "medical." A very good doctor friend once said to me: "We physicians have been kept so busy treating sicknesses and diseases, that we haven't had much time to do extensive study and research into the causes of these troubles." In God's new world, they will be given ample time for that.

In the world tomorrow there actually will be utopia. There will be universal good health.

How can such utopian dreams come true?

It's simple. Remove the cause of disease.

But how is that going to be done? Two ways:

First, by right education. Cause people to know that God did not design the human physical body so that it must be getting sick all the time, catching continual diseases. Sickness and disease occur only when nature's laws are broken. It is not natural to be diseased—it is unnatural. Educate people in the laws of good health. In proper diet. God designed certain foods for good health. Some things that grow are not designed for food. Some are poison. Educate people in sanitation, hygiene, required amounts of sleep, pure water, fresh air, sunshine, exercise.

And secondly, when people in spite of this education, do get sick or catch a disease, it can be healed—God's way. Actually, Christ's healing is forgiveness of sin. It works on a principle exactly opposite to the supposed cures of medical "science."

The medical equation is this: One poison in your body, plus one poison in the form of medicine, equals no poisons. One plus one equals nothing? That isn't the way they teach in second grade arithmetic.

God's equation is different. God supernaturally removes the poison in the body. One minus one equals nothing. The second-grader could figure that one out.

But does God, then prevent His laws of nature from working—from exacting their penalty? Oh, no—not at all. Upon repentance, and faith, God forgives the sin, and removes the penalty. How? Why? Because Jesus Himself *took*

83

our infirmities, and bare our sicknesses (Matthew 8:16-17). And Peter explains that by His *stripes* [we are] *healed* (I Peter 2:24).

Before Jesus was put to death (paying the death penalty for spiritual sin in our stead—Romans 6:23), He submitted to being beaten with stripes, thus paying in our stead the penalty of physical sin. God does not prevent His laws from working. Christ paid the penalty for us. In God's way, the penalty was paid—not nullified.

Christ said, when He observed the faith of some friends of a man with palsy, *Son, thy sins be forgiven thee* (Mark 2:5). Christ's healing is forgiveness of sin.

But when the people didn't understand such a strange statement, Christ said, *Why reason ye these things in your hearts? Whether is it easier to say to the sick of the palsy, Thy sins be forgiven thee; or to say, Arise, and take up thy bed, and walk? But that ye may know that the Son of man hath power on earth to forgive sins . . .* (Mark 2:8-10).

And when Jesus Christ becomes the great ruler of this earth, He will use that great power. In vision, John saw the angels praising Christ at His coming to rule this earth.

They said, *We give thee thanks, O Lord God Almighty, which art, and wast, and art to come; because thou hast taken to thee thy great power, and hast reigned* (Revelation 11:17).

The combined force of right education about true health, and healing of all sickness, when it is repented of, will mean perfect, utopian health.

Notice how God describes it.

But there the glorious [Eternal] *will be unto us a place of broad rivers and streams; wherein shall go no galley with oars, neither shall gallant ship pass thereby. For the* [Eternal] *is our Judge, the* [Eternal] *is our lawgiver, the* [Eternal] *is our king; He will save us.*

And the inhabitant shall not say, I am sick: the people that dwell therein shall be forgiven their iniquity (Isaiah 33:21-22, 24).

Listen to this wonderful promise: *Strengthen ye the weak hands, and confirm the feeble knees. Say to them that are of a fearful heart, Be strong, fear not: behold, your God will come with vengeance, even God with a recompence; he will come and save you. Then the eyes of the blind shall be opened, and the ears of the deaf shall be unstopped. Then shall the lame man leap as an hart, and the tongue of the dumb sing . . .* (Isaiah 35:3-6).

God describes the rewards for obedience to His laws of mercy and love. Notice Isaiah 58:8, *Then shall thy light break forth as the morning, and thine health shall spring forth speedily. . . .*

Happiness in Health

In describing the conditions of good health and plenty to be ushered in upon the earth, God says, *For I will restore health unto thee, and I will heal thee of thy wounds, saith the* [Eternal] . . . (Jeremiah 30:17).

Therefore they shall come and sing in the height of Zion, and shall flow together to the goodness of the [Eternal], *for wheat, and for wine, and for oil, and for the young of the flock and the herd: and their soul shall be as a watered garden; and they shall not sorrow any more at all.*

Then shall the virgin rejoice in the dance, both young men and old together: for I will turn their mourning into joy, and will comfort them, and make them rejoice from their sorrow. And I will satiate the soul of the priests with fatness, and my people shall be satisfied with my goodness, saith the [Eternal] (Jeremiah 31:12-14).

And why not have good health?

Why should we be so willing to believe such a perfect state of health and joy is impossible?

There are blessings for observing the laws of health—absolute guarantees good health will result—and that sickness and disease will become a thing of the past.

Notice what God promised His people, . . . *if thou shalt hearken diligently unto the voice of the* [Eternal] *thy God, to observe and to do all his commandments which I command thee this day . . . all these blessings shall come on thee, and overtake thee, if thou shalt hearken unto the voice of the* [Eternal] *thy God.*

Blessed shalt thou be in the city, and blessed shalt thou be in the field. Blessed shall be the fruit of thy body, and the fruit of thy ground, and the fruit of thy cattle, the increase of thy kine, and the flocks of thy sheep. Blessed shall be thy basket and thy store (Deuteronomy 28:1-5).

But we are not receiving those wonderful blessings today.

Instead, we are under a curse!

Our cities are festering sores, filled with the clangor and confusion of jangled traffic, riots, racial hatred, crime, pornography, air pollution, and an unhappy, wretched populace that seeks fast money so it can escape the obnoxious environment of the big asphalt and concrete "jungles" of our time!

Our fields are cursed; cursed with upset weather, drought, flood, insect damage and disease—cursed with chemicals and man-made blight.

One out of fourteen of the babies born in the United States are illegitimate, and in Chicago, Cleveland and Houston, it's one out of ten—and of the total babies born each year, over six percent are blighted at birth with a serious defect; cursed with blindness, dumbness, deafness, malformed limbs, or terrible diseases even from the womb. Some babies are born each year with cancer!

Our *basket* and our *store* is cursed—depleted national reserves—gone overseas to feed starving peoples (to nations which rarely, if ever, back U.S. policies) in an admittedly temporary effort—only delaying the starvation facing millions.

Whether we like to admit it or not—our peoples are under a curse today.

But soon, the great God will force us to take the blessings. He will impose His warm and merciful rule on rebellious, stiff-necked mankind, and bring us compulsory joy. He will insist on happiness for us; demand plenty of goodness in our lives; command us to be healthy, and filled with a sense of well-being and contentment.

And so the frightening, manifold problems of the population explosion, bad weather, sickness and disease, and all problems relating to the population rise—such as overcrowding, pollution, rising crime, and the psychological pressures from big-city living—all these will be solved—and in our time.

What about Distribution of Populations?

Will there be room for the multiple billions of humans on earth?

Of course. Remember, only 15 percent of the earth's surface is habitable today—and not more than 10 percent is cultivatable. But when God makes all the earth inhabitable, even changing the whole weather patterns of earth, the ocean currents, and flow of arctic air, the jet streams, the pattern of mountain ranges and placement of continents, all earth will be peopled.

God shows individual races returning to their own lands, repopulating them. *He shall cause them that come of Jacob to take root: Israel shall blossom and bud,*

87

and fill the face of the world with fruit (Isaiah 27:6).

God says the wastes will be rebuilt.

For behold, I am for you, and I will turn unto you and ye shall be tilled and sown: and I will multiply men upon you, all the house of Israel, even all of it: and the cities shall be inhabited, and the wastes shall be builded: And I will multiply upon you man and beast; and they shall increase and bring fruit: and I will settle you after your old estates . . . (Ezekiel 36:9-11).

Read the whole chapter of Ezekiel 36. God says, *. . . I will also cause you to dwell in the cities, and the wastes shall be builded . . . This land that was desolate is become like the Garden of Eden; and the waste and desolate and ruined cities are become fenced, and are inhabited* (verses 33, 35).

And what about all other nations?

Notice, *In that day shall there be a highway out of Egypt* [Egypt still exists as a nation] *to Assyria* [many of whose people migrated centuries ago to northcentral Europe—modern Germany], *and the Assyrian shall come into Egypt, and the Egyptian into Assyria, and the Egyptians shall serve with the Assyrians. In that day shall Israel be the third with Egypt and with Assyria, even a blessing in the midst of the land: whom the* [Eternal] *of hosts shall bless, saying, Blessed be Egypt my people, and Assyria, the work of my hands, and Israel mine inheritance* (Isaiah 19:23-25).

What a utopian prediction that is!

Egypt and Germany are pictured in loving, respectful, serving cooperation with the very peoples they contended with in the past.

That's real progress!

So your Bible reveals nations still existing—and in specific places. It reveals repopulation of waste places rendered temporarily useless by the ravages of war and plagues.

88

7

...And All Speaking the Same Language

Can you imagine a world of one language? Think back a little. One of the major barriers to mutual understanding and cooperation between peoples has been the language barrier. When one man cannot understand another— he can't freely exchange ideas, philosophies, concepts, or opinions. And in translating, the personal rapport, the sense and feeling of what is being said, is lost.

If you have ever experienced talking to someone through an interpreter, you probably remember how awkward you felt.

Today, this world stands on the brink of cosmocide. Great races, having different languages, cannot seem to come to a meeting of minds. And different peoples' minds work differently.

A different language means a different culture, different music, different habits, different education, different values and standards, and a whole different approach to life.

Fantastic Illiteracy

Think what an almost unbelievable step forward it would be, if all peoples everywhere spoke, and read, and wrote the same language.

But today, vast areas of the earth do not even possess a written language. Millions upon millions are illiterate—cannot read or write, even their own names.

Millions of others are sadly limited in expressing themselves, even in their own language—and haven't bothered to learn the language of another people.

One of the great handicaps to free trade, to the exchange of ideas and cultural thought, is the language barrier.

If the language barrier were removed—and everyone became totally literate—with fine minds, grasping the same thoughts, capable of thinking the same terms, capable of understanding each other fully—think of the huge changes that could be effected.

First, consider what a universal worldwide language would mean today, with the world cut off from God.

Evils would multiply. Universally there would be a new age in art (pornography), in perverted literature, Godless education, Satan-inspired music—such as the U.S. and Britain are spawning over the world now—of quarreling and hostility and war between nations.

Such evils beginning at the Tower of Babel caused God to confound the languages, to prevent such evils from spreading through direct communication between peoples and nations.

90

But, in the world tomorrow with God's civilization established, and ruled by Christ—what a blessing it will be.

Man was once bound together by a common tongue. But he used his knowledge for evil—for an attempt to begin the very civilization that would end by destroying itself.

When God divided the languages at the tower of Babel, He was merely forestalling that eventual time of world chaos which even now threatens the annihilation of humanity.

But once the returning Christ conquers this earth, He will usher in an era of total literacy, total education—and give the world one, new, pure, language.

This subject by itself needs a book to describe. The whole literary processes of the whole earth changed. Today, all languages are corrupt. They are literally filled with pagan, heathen terms—superstition—misnomers—exceptions to rules—peculiar idioms.

In our English language, Germanic in origin but with a great deal borrowed from Latin (either directly or through French) and other languages, there are many such terms we take for granted.

"Romance" comes from "Roman"—because that's what the Romans did. People are called "lunatics" because of an old superstition that the moon (Latin *luna*) caused insanity. Some "thank their lucky stars," a holdover from astrology (which more and more of our "enlightened" society are turning to). Others even still use pagan curses such as "by Jove."

Our rockets (Thor, Agena, Atlas, Titan) are named after pagan gods and goddesses of the Greeks and Romans, and our space programs (Gemini, Apollo) are named the same way.

June brides want to get married under the sign of the

91

ancient goddess of fertility (though it's not chic to have large families any more), and our days and months bear pagan names.

All languages have peculiarities of expression and grammatical oddities which cause misunderstandings and make them difficult for foreigners to learn. In most cases, even native speakers have problems with their own language, as Professor Higgins so astutely observed in *My Fair Lady*. Many are in sad need of spelling reform, English being probably the prime example (*ough* has about six different possible pronunciations). The modes of writing vary from Chinese, which still uses a form of picture writing, to a multiplicity of different alphabets, including Greek, Arabic, Sanskrit, Hebrew, and Russian. Something must be done.

God says, *For then will I turn to the people a pure language, that they may all call upon the name of the* [Eternal], *to serve Him with one consent* (Zephaniah 3:9).

Think of the new era of good literature, good music, and of the avoiding of duplicated effort, misunderstandings through linguistic difficulties and thousands of painstaking hours of translations. What an age it will be, when all the world becomes truly educated—and speaks the same language. Imagine what an affect that will have on world commerce!

What About the Economic Structure?

God shows Jerusalem will become the financial capital of earth.

The Creator says, of the newly built city, *Then thou shalt see, and flow together, and thine heart shall fear, and be enlarged; because the abundance of the sea* [the world's gold and silver reserves are mostly under the seas] *shall be converted unto thee, and the forces* [wealth, margin] *of the Gentiles shall come unto thee* (Isaiah 60:5).

92

And what vast wealth there is in the sea. The Dow Chemical Company, manufacturers of about 500 substances taken directly from seawater, say one cubic mile of seawater stores 175 million tons of dissolved chemicals worth five billion dollars.

Each cubic mile of seawater contains 93 million dollars worth of gold and eight and one-half million dollars worth of silver.

Each cubic mile contains seven tons of uranium, and enough other minerals, elements and chemicals in disolution to make each cubic mile worth, in today's figures, five billion dollars.

It's been estimated the total value of the oceans would amount to one quintillion, five hundred quadrillion dollars.

A quadrillion dollars means a thousand trillion. And a trillion is one thousand billion. A billion is one thousand million. And a million is one thousand thousand. So a quintillion is one thousand quadrillions of dollars.

This is in the waters of the seas, alone.

But, as you've already read, God Almighty says He'll raise many places now covered by waters of the oceans; that He'll make much more land available. Scientists know most of the earth's raw materials lie in the strata beneath the depths of the seas.

God says this vast wealth will become available for constructive use during the reign of Jesus Christ on this earth.

God says the wealth of the world will be centered in Jerusalem, and that the vast rebuilding programs, rehabilitation processes and new-age pioneering that begin will be backed by that wealth.

. . . Yet once, it is a little while, and I will shake the heavens, and the earth, and the sea, and the dry land: And I

93

will shake all nations, and the desire [desirable things, margin] *of all nations shall come: and I will fill this house with glory, saith the* [Eternal] *of hosts. The silver is mine, and the gold is mine, saith the* [Eternal] *of hosts* (Haggai 2:6-8).

But God's great treasury will be for public display.

No gold bricks, reposing in deep, subterranean vaults—utterly useless except for their meaning—no fear of thievery, or robbery. But breathtakingly beautiful decorations for the Capitol building, the temple in which Christ will dwell.

The gold standard will be set up; and values will never change.

No more speculating or gambling on other people's ability.

Never again will any person become rich from investing in the labors and creative ability of another person. No more stock markets, world banks, financing centers, insurance companies, mortgage companies, loan agencies, or time payments.

In God's abundant Government people will buy only what they need, when they can afford it, when they have the cash to pay for it. No more interest. And no more taxes.

But the tithing system will be universal.

Today's governments demand 20 percent; up to 40, 50, and even 90 percent in inheritance taxes, income taxes, hidden taxes; federal, state, county, school board, and city taxes.

But God requires only ten percent. And out of that ten percent will be financed the entire governmental, educational, and spiritual leadership of the whole earth.

Will a man rob God? Yet ye have robbed me. But ye say, Wherein have we robbed thee? [And God answers] *In tithes and offerings. Ye are cursed with a curse: for ye have robbed me, even this whole nation. Bring ye all the tithes into the storehouse, that there may be meat in mine house, and prove me now herewith, saith the* [Eternal] *of hosts, if I will not open you the windows of heaven, and pour you out a blessing, that there shall not be room enough to receive it* (Malachi 3:8-10). That's a prophecy for now.

And what a blessing that will be. None of the financial burdens that curse most peoples today.

People will not, then, try to "keep up with the Joneses," so they will not try to live beyond their means.

They will be educated to resist impulse buying, and lustful acquisition of various gadgets, toys, playthings, and luxury items that they can't afford, and don't need.

Take the commercialism of various holidays away— expose the true origin of pagan holidays—and people would have more money for the essentials of life that really count.

Reduce the really big expenses in most people's homes; take away all the taxes, real and hidden. Take away property taxes, school taxes (since all education will then be handled by the Family of God, and the physical family of Levi) and all other taxes; cut down totally on any medical bills (only small fees for first aid, or child delivery, or necessary physical helps), and insure no one ever again signs a 36-month contract at up to 35 or 40 percent interest on an ancient used car that falls apart while the buyer still owes more than the car is worth.

Do these things, and the financial curses under which most people live will be healed.

God says financial blessings are to become the order of the day.

Take away thievery, robbery, accidents, weather damage, rust, rot and decay from plants, stores, manufacturing concerns. How much less could merchandise then sell for— and at how much greater profits?

95

Take away weather problems, insect damage, blight and fungus from farmers—losses through government price controls and overflooding of markets—and what would be their lot in life?

Take away massive, assembly-line production of cheap, flimsy automobiles, and what would that do to solve the traffic snarls, the smog problems, the collisions and loss of life and the whole social and economic picture?

God will accomplish these things.

How will He do so?

First, by changing the nature of human beings; changing their outlook toward life, removing their lust and selfishness, their covetousness and greed that drives them onward toward material goals.

And how will that be done? By putting away the super-powerful Satan, the prince of the power of the air—the spirit being that now is working in deceived, misled, human beings (Eph. 2:2; Rev. 20:1-3). Satan is the source of human nature, which humans acquire from him.

James says, *Do ye think that the scripture saith in vain, The spirit that dwelleth in us lusts to envy?* (James 4:5). And Jeremiah was inspired to write, *The heart is deceitful above all things, and desperately wicked: who can know it?* (Jeremiah 17:9).

Human nature covets. It lusts for the things money can buy. It longs for prestige, recognition, admiration and popularity. It lusts for power, position, wealth.

Ask any segment of our modern-day populations what they desire most in life, and they'll almost invariably answer, "money"! Actually, they want the things money can buy. They know prestige and recognition come through the acquisition of material goods. They know most people evaluate other people by what they possess—by the kind of clothing

96

they wear, the kind of home in which they live, the kind of automobiles they drive, and the material goods they possess.

No wonder God says, *. . . godliness with contentment is great gain. For we brought nothing into this world, and it is certain we can carry nothing out. And having food and raiment let us be therewith content* (I Timothy 6:6-8).

Christ commanded, *Lay not up for yourselves treasures upon earth, where moth and rust doth corrupt, and where thieves break through and steal: But lay up for yourselves treasures in heaven, where neither moth nor rust doth corrupt, and where thieves do not break through nor steal: for where your treasure is, there will your heart be also* (Matthew 6:19-21).

He said, *Therefore take no* [anxious, worried, concerned] *thought, saying, What shall we eat? or . . . Wherewithal shall we be clothed? (For after all these things do the Gentiles seek:) for your heavenly Father knoweth that ye have need of these things. But seek ye first the Kingdom of God* [His soon-coming, righteous government on this earth, which very government, and its results this book is explaining], *and his righteousness; and all these things shall be added unto you* (Matthew 6:31-33).

Notice. It is not a sin to be rich. But it is a sin to covet riches, or to put your heart on material things.

Our God is a multibillionaire heavenly Father. *The gold is mine* He says (Hag. 2:8).

And God wants every child of His to truly prosper. *Beloved, I wish above all things that thou mayest prosper and be in health . . .* (III John 2). Christ said, *I am come that they might have life, and that they might have it more abundantly* (John 10:10).

God wants fullness, abundance in every life.

But look at the material "successes" you've known. How truly happy are they? As J. Paul Getty, one of the world's richest men, is reputed to have said, "I'd give all my millions for just one happy marriage!"

In God's Kingdom, these commands of His will be obeyed. They'll become the standard for regulating commerce, business, finance, and the entire economic structure of the world.

And all will be on the giving basis. Christ said, *Give, and it shall be given unto you; good measure, pressed down, and shaken together, and running over, shall men give into your bosom. For with the same measure that ye mete withal it shall be measured to you again* (Luke 6:38).

The giving standard will be followed in God's rule on this earth—not the grasping, conniving, striving, deceitful, clandestine, furtive, scurrilous, devious, cheating and lying chicanery that is commonplace in today's business world.

Look at the corruption in the world through lust for money. It's no wonder God says, . . . *they that will be rich fall into temptation and a snare, and into many foolish and hurtful lusts, which drown men in destruction and perdition. For the love of money is a root of all evils* [correct translation] . . . (I Timothy 6:9-10).

But when God converts rebellious mankind by the display of His mighty power—when He brings to pass His promise; *As I live, saith the* [Eternal], *every knee shall bow to me, and every tongue shall confess to God* (Romans 14:11), when He humbles the vain, proud spirit of man—then man will be made willing to give.

And until God breaks the haughty spirit of man (Isaiah 2:10-12, 17)—the peoples of earth will not be ready to accept such a wonderful, loving, generous, honest giving standard for the whole economy.

98

It would require a thick book to begin to describe the wonderful conditions which could prevail on this earth—and which will finally prevail, when the human heart is humbled, converted—given the very nature of God (II Peter 1:4).

Never again will anyone build a building he can't afford, and doesn't need, to lease and rent to tenants who help him pay for it. No more interest. God says it is sin to lend money at "usury" or interest.

Once each fifty years, all debts, public and private, will be cancelled, completely.

Since governments will be in the hands of the spiritual Family of God, and partially administered by those human leaders directly under that great ruling Family—and since there will be no huge bureaus watching other huge bureaus, which are suspiciously watching other bureaus; no military establishment; no FBI, CIA, or members of Interpol; no huge cartels, monopolies, unions, or giant government spending—the economy of the world will be healed.

Think of it. No more foreign aid—none of the wasted billions to buy "lovers" (allies) (Ezekiel 23:9, 22; Lamentations 1:2, 19; Ezekiel, 16th chapter) who turn and rend you later. No more government grants to industry, to science and space technology, to schools and institutions for research.

Instead, every necessary industry, educational institution, and business will be in sound financial condition.

What a world that will be!

Final Summation

Statesmen, scientists, educators know the only hope for survival and for peace is one world government. We could quote many scores of world leaders affirming this.

We could quote other scores of world leaders saying it is impossible.

So it's "world government—or annihilation" on the one hand, and it's "world government is impossible" on the other hand.

That is the stark paradox of terror facing all mankind today. No wonder God Almighty says *the way of peace have they not known* (Rom. 3:17).

But what man cannot do for himself, the Great Living God will do for him. World government—perfect government—is coming in our time, in the hands of the Great Ruling Christ, and unnumbered thousands of Co-Rulers given immortality with and under Him.

And that good news is the true Gospel of Jesus Christ. Christ is to inherit the world throne (Luke 1:32-33), which God had promised to David would never cease on this earth (II Samuel 7:13). Jesus said, before Pilate, it was for this express purpose that He was born (John 18:36-37).

Jesus constantly preached the good news about the coming Kingdom of God (Matthew 4:23; 6:10; 7:21; Mark 1:15; 4:11; 14:25; Luke 4:43; 8:10; 9:2, 11, 62, etc.). He pictured Himself as the young nobleman going away (to heaven) to be coronated, and to return to earth (Luke 19:12-27).

Repeatedly Jesus said He would return to earth (Matthew 24:27, 30-31, 42; 25:13; Mark 13:26; Luke 12:42-43; 17:24; 18:8; 19:12; 21:27; John 14:3, etc.). *If I go and prepare a place* [position, office, habitation] *for you, I will come again, and receive you unto myself, that where I am, there ye may be also* (John 14:3). He will then be in the clouds and on the earth—Zechariah 14:3-4 with I Thessalonians 4:16-17.

The living Christ is coming in all the power and glory of Almighty God, as *King of kings and Lord of lords* (Revelation 19:11-21), to put down the rebellion of warring nations

100

(Revelation 17:14), and establish God's world-ruling Government over all nations (Daniel 2:44; 7:9, 13-14, 18, 22-27; Isaiah 9:7).

No wonder the whole hope of a true Christian is the resurrection (Acts 23:6; 24:15) to immortality—eternal life—as a co-ruler, under Christ. Jesus said: *And he that overcometh, and keepeth my works unto the end, to him will I give power over the nations: and he shall rule them with a rod of iron . . .* (Revelation 2:26-27). And again, *To him that overcometh will I grant to sit with me in my throne* [on this earth] (Revelation 3:21; Luke 1:32-33). And . . . *we shall reign on the earth* (Revelation 5:10).

The Apostle John, in vision, saw a preview of the beginning of that rule and world government: *I saw thrones, and they sat upon them, and judgment was given unto them . . . and they lived and reigned with Christ a thousand years* (Revelation 20:4).

Jesus said no one could see or enter into the Kingdom of God until he is born of God (John 3:3-5). He made plain when one is born of God, he, just as God is, will be Spirit. We have now, as humans, been born of flesh—and therefore we are flesh. But God is Spirit (John 4:24, RSV), and when we are born of God—of the Spirit—we shall be Spirit (John 3:6-8). Now, we are earthy—of the earth (I Corinthians 15:48). We are "flesh and blood" from the earth—from matter (verse 50)—yet flesh and blood humans cannot inherit the Kingdom of God (same verse). But, as we have borne the image of the earthy—mortal—human—we shall, when born of God, bear the image of the heavenly that is, spirit (verse 49).

Christ, the King of kings. Perfect in character, absolute in honesty, integrity, faithfulness, loyalty and trust; filled with outgoing concern for the governed—their welfare and

101

salvation; total knowledge, understanding, wisdom. Complete love, mercy, patience, kindness, compassion, forgiveness. Yet, possessing total power, and never compromising one millionth of an inch with His perfect law—which is the way of love. He will enforce God's Law—God's government on earth. He will compel haughty, carnal, rebellious humans to yield in complete submission to God's Government.

No one will be deceived—as the vast majority of mankind is today. All will know the truth. No more religious confusion. Eyes will be opened to the truth. Humans will become teachable. People will start living God's way—the way of outgoing concern for others—the way of the true values—the way of peace, of happiness, of well-being, of joy.

Crime, sickness, disease, pain and suffering, gone. Poverty, ignorance banished. Smiles on people's faces—faces that radiate. Wild animals tame. Air pollution, water pollution, soil pollution, gone. Crystal pure water to drink; clean, crisp, pure air to breathe; rich black soil where deserts, mountains and seas formerly were, producing full-flavored foods, and fantastic beauty in flowers, shrubs, trees. A world filled with happy radiating humans, guided, helped, protected, and ruled by former mortals made immortal—and all the humans realizing that they, too, may inherit everlasting life in supreme happiness and thrilling joy.

What a fabulous picture!

For further reading on topics briefly discussed in this book, the following titles by Herbert W. Armstrong are available in booklet form free of charge:

Does God Exist?
The Seven Laws of Success
Why Were You Born?
What Do You Mean—Born Again?
What Is The True Gospel?

Simply write to:

The Worldwide Church of God
Box 111
Pasadena, California 91123

Index

Scripture Index

108